I have known Dan Taylor for over 25 years and have always been motivated and challenged by his heart for those with alcohol and drug addictions. We served together on the board of Trinity Mission for 15 of those years. His real passion is for uniting the larger body of Christ in ministry to those with addictions. This book is a culmination of his work to seek mentors from local churches to help the recovering addict in their spiritual walk with Christ and to help them return to productive members of society. This book will be invaluable to anyone that desires to help those with addictions. Praise the Lord for this endeavor.

Harry Latshaw
Former Board Member Elder at The Living Stone Church

Dan Taylor knows about the "seasons of change" in a person's life, changes he has experienced in his own life. As a result, he has walked many people, caught in addictions, to freedom. I have been amazed at the amount of understanding and wisdom and helpful direction Dan has received, something he feels is from the Lord and His Word. He has taken these insights and liberally shared them with needy people. Consequently, many have been set free so they can be transformed into what God intended for them. Dan also carries a burden to help men be God's ambassadors in leading their families in truth and wisdom and the enjoyment of a godly family.

Delmar Broersma Upper Room Christian Fellowship

Seasons of Change

Freedom from the Imprisonment of the Past

DANIEL L. TAYLOR

WESTBOW
PRESS®
A DIVISION OF THOMAS NELSON
& ZONDERVAN

WestBow Press books may be ordered through booksellers or by contacting:

WestBow Press
A Division of Thomas Nelson & Zondervan
1663 Liberty Drive
Bloomington, IN 47403
www.westbowpress.com
1 (866) 928-1240

ISBN: 978-1-5127-6819-0 (sc)
ISBN: 978-1-5127-6818-3 (e)

Library of Congress Control Number: 2016920648

Print information available on the last page.

WestBow Press rev. date: 1/3/2017

"Seasons of Change" is a unique and effective approach to finding freedom from addictions and behavioral struggles. It is based solely upon over 25 years of experience ministering to those addicted and helping each individual to find freedom through Jesus Christ and the local members of a Church. More than anything else, it is through this approach that I found freedom and wholeness myself.

One of the most important suggestions that I can make has three elements to act upon.

<u>**First**</u> – be totally honest, transparent and without reservation with yourself and at least one other within the Church God chooses for you, hopefully your mentor. The most important bench mark for someone seeking freedom through Jesus Christ is being honest with yourself.

<u>**Second**</u> – keep attending the Church God has chosen for you, once you have begun this journey. Satan tries to steal, kill and destroy and his main instrument is dividing the Body of Christ. Don't allow him that satisfaction. I have instructed the myriad of those I have ministered to over these years with these two simple actions if you are considering leaving the Church for another – first – spend time writing down why you want to leave and speak with the Pastor and your mentor face-to-face, giving them a chance to respond to your complaint or reason – second – if they cannot show you it is better to stay than to leave, agree to stay for another two months before leaving. Ask God what He wants during that time and listen to His response.

<u>**Third**</u> – and perhaps the most important thing to do to gain life-long freedom, keep this workbook and all your notes. Each year, go back over the responses you make, considering that same question or response and responding once again. Then look back on that previous year and ask God and your own heart (your mentor also) – *have I made progress during the past year?*

Discipleship is about long term growth toward Christ-likeness over your entire time on this earth. The problems and control this struggle has over everyone plagued by it did not start quickly, and it will not be totally over quickly either. By doing this year after year, you will be pleased to see how well you are doing and God will bless your efforts with signs of His pleasure!

Contents

Preface

Seasons of Change – winter, spring, summer, fall – brings a parallel to the design God has for the "seasons" of weather as it relates to gardening or growing those plants that nourish us. It also brings a pattern for the changes He calls for us to make in our spiritual growth. The primary focus of this workbook is on changing from addictions of all types - - chemicals and behaviors - - but the model and principles apply to all of life. I should confess that while I enjoy growing plants, I seldom am engaged in the actual "dirt work," but consistently engaged in the consuming of the results.

In agricultural circles the simple description of what is a priority in each season applies to this analogous journey to freedom from addictions and growth in Jesus, the Christ.

Winter – a time to evaluate the quality and quantity of the "fruit" of the labors. Has the best possible nutritional value been accomplished, were the seeds or seedlings the right choice, has the pattern and layout of the garden been most productive, was it well tended and was the balance of what was invested what is needed for the best nourishment?

Spring – a time to prepare the soil, add nutrients and select seed and plant varieties to meet the goals desired. Are extra soil additives needed, have all the weed seeds been removed, have rocks and other debris been extracted, at what soil temperature is it best to plant, and finally, has the soil been tilled to prepare for the best possible future fruit?

Summer – the time for caring well for what has been sown. A time to pull weeds, to water when rainfall is less than enough, a time to till the soil to prevent it from hardening. A time to be on the lookout for varmints that should be driven away and damaging invasions of insect or fungus, is the sun too hot for proper growth or does shade need to be provided? Do nutrients need to be added for the best possible growth? Sometimes pruning and shaping needs to be done for the best possible outcomes.

Fall – the harvest season. This is a time of watching for ripening produce, picking what is ready and patiently waiting and watching for the next time of picking, cleaning and preparing the fruit for preservation for the future, trimming back the unneeded growth and amending the soil so the winter rest will prepare for the next spring.

God created heavens and earth, man and woman, plants and animals and He designed them all to work in harmony for one ultimate goal – His glory. The animals and plants were for man's dominion and provision so every human could be in an ever deepening relationship with Him.

"There is an appointed time for everything. And there is a time for every event under heaven, A time to give birth and a time to die; A time to plant and a time to uproot what is planted. A time to kill and a time to heal; A time to tear down and a time to build up. A time to weep and a time to laugh; A time to mourn and a time to dance. A time to throw stones and a time to gather stones; A time to embrace and a time to shun embracing. A time to search and a time to give up as lost; A time to keep and a time to throw away. A time to tear apart and a time to sew together; A time to be silent and a time to speak. A time to love and a time to hate; A time for war and a time for peace. What profit is there to the worker from that in which he toils? I have seen the task which God has given the sons of men with which to occupy themselves."
Ecclesiastes 3:1 – 9 (NASB)

Introduction

When we turn to solutions for life's issues outside of the way we are designed to resolve them, problems inevitably result. Some of the consequences are relatively minor and can easily be remedied, while other consequences result in a much more destructive outcome.

Loneliness, stress at work or in our relationships, anger, escape from physical and emotional pain – all these and a myriad of other "life issues" are difficult to handle. When those difficulties begin to become more than we can bear, we seek solutions that are close and seemingly easy to access. A drink or two, a few tokes on a joint or a pain pill. Perhaps a friend or acquaintance has suggested meth or speed or a sexual liaison. With that first experience we find some relief and, often, no consequences, even though it was wrong. Even if the substance or behavior is legal or not viewed as unacceptable or terrible by society's standards, it still seems wrong deep within.

Life gets somewhat back to "normal" and then those same stressors or others problems come along. We try other ways to deal with them but nothing brings relief. Our minds or someone in our sphere of relationships suggests taking that same escape route again. We give in and the stress relief works, at least for a while. As life goes on the stressors continue and the escape route is used more frequently. Even during times when there is little or no stress, just idle time or a sense of wanting some recreational activity comes along and we turn to our "old pal," whatever it is.

More and more we turn to our "old pal" as a means of escape or recreation, as a way to deal with boredom or simply because we enjoy the way it makes us feel. The frequency and magnitude begins to increase and, seemingly out of nowhere, we find ourselves thinking about our means of escape often throughout the day and evening.

Soon our thoughts are literally focused more on the substance or the behavior than on anything else. We begin to rationalize by thinking we are still in control and can stop anytime. Even the others around us may support the idea that we are still in control and can stop at any time. We lie to ourselves and others who confront us with the addiction, which we never acknowledge is an addiction when deep inside, we know it is an addiction.

It begins to impact our finances, our jobs, and our relationships. If we ever stop to think of our life and our thinking and actions, it feels deep inside as if our brains and lives have been hijacked. We are locked in a prison and cannot find the way out. Why do we feel this way and how did it happen? The answers are at the same time simple and complex - - physical and emotional and, most importantly - - spiritual in nature. More detailed information will be provided later.

What is most important to establish here and now is that there is a way out of this prison! There is a way to prevent us from being hijacked again. That way is through significant relationships being established and us being deeply committed to them for our journey into freedom.

Understanding How

All relationships eventually take one of several possible courses. Some, hopefully many, become committed and significant and develop over time into deep, long lasting and trusting relationships. The various depths of trust and closeness in all relationships are impacted by a wide variety of situations and circumstances. As with life itself, the richness and fullness of these relationships are determined by many things, most of which are within the control of each one in the relationship. The most predominate and influential of those factors are our individual choices and actions. Of the many choices we face in an ongoing relationship, openness, honesty, transparency, and genuineness are extremely important. Those factors are what determine the amount of trust and mutual respect each person in the relationship has for the other. That trust develops when integrity is demonstrated over time in that relationship and is negatively impacted when that integrity is damaged.

Each one involved in the relationship is able to grow in his or her ability to be progressively more open and transparent, when he or she chooses to. The cycle continues until it reaches a degree of transparency and openness that fosters a clear and vivid understanding of the fruit in such a relationship, which, in turn, brings complete genuineness. That understanding and the resulting benefits of increased openness and transparency to the relationship provides even more freedom for both parties. In that very environment of a constantly growing trust and complete safety for both individuals, those imprisoned by addictions can begin to be set free as never before.

That is also true with the most significant relationship of all – the relationship with God the Father through Jesus Christ, the Son. When integrity and openness are the foundational principles of that relationship, freedom comes in abundance.

"O Lord, who may abide in Your tent? Who may dwell on Your holy hill? He who walks with integrity, and works righteousness, And speaks truth in his heart." Psalm 15:1&2(NASB)

The safest environment and the only relationship that will bring complete and total freedom from addictions and all other forms of bondage is found in a relationship with JESUS CHRIST. Without a relationship with JESUS CHRIST in the process of learning to live life free from addictions and compulsions, there is no true freedom.

"So if the Son makes you free, you will be free indeed." John 8:36 (NASB)"

"It was for freedom that Christ set us free; therefore keep standing firm and do not be subject again to a yoke of slavery." Galatians 5:1 (NASB)

Total and complete freedom from controlling behaviors and addictions can best be understood when compared to the two types of freedom experienced when early release from a prison sentence is given.

When someone is pardoned, the crime's consequences are completely eliminated. No further consequences are awaiting them unless they act in a criminal manner again. Many times the actual crime can be taken off the record, should the person exhibit a changed attitude and ask forgiveness of the judge. When people are paroled from prison, although they may have completed their sentence, the consequences of that sentence are hanging over their heads. Should they choose to violate a different law or violate any of the court orders, they are often returned to prison. If the violation is serious enough, a paroled person could be required to serve the full amount of prison originally imposed.

When individuals are paroled from prison, they feel the weight of the burden of their sentence on their day-to-day lives. If they commit even one mistake of the slightest magnitude, they are likely going to be returned to prison to serve the remainder of their sentence.

When the same individuals are pardoned by the legal system for the same offense, the sentence is immediately completed and they are free to live life without the worry of a minor mistake sending them back.

Freedom from addictions and controlling behaviors through a genuine and transparent relationship with Jesus Christ is the same as receiving a pardon. Without the Savior, it carries the same fear and tentative nature as a parole.

When people are imprisoned by substance abuse or by behaviors that are unacceptable and they are unable to see a way of escape, there should be a point where they admit they need help.

At that time it is critical to find the power and strength to break the chains of all that imprisons us, otherwise we will destroy ourselves and those around us. The cry of every heart is "freedom" and now, once the admission is made, that cry is louder and stronger than the hijacker that has held us hostage.

God loves His people and wants everyone to accept Him as Father, through His Son Jesus Christ. Second to that love, He loves it when someone cries out to Him – ***"I am weak and need You and Your strength to set me free from this prison! I want to turn my life around and live the way I should, the way You designed me to live!"***

That act, with those words, when cried out honestly is simply what is called repentance. To repent simply means that you agree you are doing what God doesn't approve of and you want to turn around and do what He does approve of. In that cry you are also confessing that you need God's help, His strength and power, because you are doing what you don't truly want to do and feel powerless to stop it. Confession and repentance truly bring joy to God's heart. He does not think less of us when we cry out in confession and repentance. He thinks more of us! His desire for all mankind is that it will be in honest relationship with Him and will be quick to admit it is wrong. God wants all of His creation to live in open, honest and transparent relationship with Him.

"The LORD your God is in your midst, A victorious warrior. He will exult over you with joy,

He will be quiet in His love, He will rejoice over you with shouts of joy." Zephaniah 3:17 (NASB)

"If we confess our sins, He is faithful and righteous to forgive us our sins and to cleanse us from all unrighteousness." John 1:9 (NASB)

There is no better time than right now to spend some time talking with God and admitting we have been hijacked and cannot get free through our own power. The drugs and behaviors that have taken us prisoner have more power than we have in our own strength. Believe it or not, this condition has existed since the first man and woman on earth went against God's design for them. Even the greatest apostle of all time, Paul, struggled with doing what he didn't want to do and not doing what he knew was pleasing to God.

"For we know that the Law is spiritual, but I am of flesh, sold into bondage to sin. For what I am doing, I do not understand; for I am not practicing what I would like to do, but I am doing the very thing I hate. But if I do the very thing I do not want to do, I agree with the Law, confessing that the Law is good. So now, no longer am I the one doing it, but sin which dwells in me. For I know that nothing good dwells in me, that is, in my flesh; for the willing is present in me, but the doing of the good is not. For the good that I want, I do not do, but I practice the very evil that I do not want. But if I am doing the very thing I do not want, I am no longer the one doing it, but sin which dwells in me.

I find then the principle that evil is present in me, the one who wants to do good. For I joyfully concur with the law of God in the inner man, but I see a different law in the members of my body, waging war against the law of my mind and making me a prisoner of the law of sin which is in my members. Wretched man that I am! Who will set me free from the body of this death? Thanks be to God through Jesus Christ our Lord! So then, on the one hand I myself with my mind am serving the law of God, but on the other, with my flesh the law of sin."

Romans 7:14 – 25 (NASB)

Are you willing? The answer to that question should be yes, because you are reading this and something is happening within your heart. The question most important now is one only you can answer. "Why are you willing and why are you reading this material? What is your motivation for change?" Take some time right now and write out how you are feeling, emotionally and spiritually as well as your thoughts. Remember, no one but you will read this, unless you choose to share it. You are totally safe to write your true feelings and thoughts!!

_____

_____

_____

_____

_____

_____

_____

_____

_____

_____

_____

_____

_____

_____

_____

_____

_____

_____

_____

_____

_____

_____

_____

_____

_____

_____

_____

_____

_____

_____

_____

_____

_____

Now that you have written your feelings and thoughts out, set that aside, take a break and, while you feel as if your emotions are stable and you are feeling well, pray about this issue. Ask God through the Holy Spirit to share His true heart with you and ask Him to let you know how loved you are by Him. You are deeply loved and totally forgiven for what you confessed.

Fruits of The Past

Take some time and honestly and transparently write a sentence or two to explain why you are willing to consider this approach to freedom. Be honest – is it because you want freedom and are sick and tired of life going the way it has been – or, did someone else require you to get help and threaten you with something if you didn't get help somewhere? Perhaps someone threatened to terminate your relationship or threatened to make you homeless and without support. Whatever the reason, write it out so you can see it and say it to yourself, if not to God.

_____

_____

_____

_____

_____

Whatever the reason, be encouraged by even considering this approach. It is no coincidence to God, because He never allows a coincident! He always places people and circumstances together so choices can be made - - choices between Him and His ways or man and his ways. He is a gentleman and never forces Himself upon anyone, that is why there is so many problems in the world. God could easily overpower all the violence and depravity, but He wants people to willing choose Him.

It is also not a bad thing to admit our weakness and our need to seek help from others and God. Many very strong people in the history of the world have admitted they are wrong, weak and in need of help from God and others. It is not a sign of a lack of intelligence either. In history many extremely educated people were addicted to substances or behaviors that are unacceptable to God. He allowed them to suffer from serious consequences of their disobedience because of His "tough love" for His people.

To help understand what has happened that brought you to this point, read and write how each of these different circumstances looked in your life. Begin the practice of being totally open, honest, and transparent with yourself. The items written in this exercise will only be shared by you, when you choose and with whom you choose.

List all the drugs / alcohol / behaviors (not acceptable to the Lord) you have been involved with.

_____

_____

_____

_____

_____

How old were you **when** you first engaged in behaviors not acceptable to the Lord? _____

How old were you **when** you first drank alcohol in any quantity? _____

How old were you **when** you first used drugs in any quantity?_____

What are **your thoughts** on **why** you first drank or used drugs or participated in the behaviors?

_____

_____

_____

_____

_____

_____

_____

_____

_____

What are your thoughts on why you continued drinking / using/ participating in the behaviors?

_____

_____

_____

_____

_____

Describe the patterns of your use of drugs/alcohol/participating in these behaviors in your own words. List the frequency (daily – 4 times a day – weekly – 2 times a week, etc) and the amount / quantity. Try to remember as accurately as possible.

_____

_____

_____

_____

_____

Has there ever been a time when you used alcohol / drugs or participated in the behaviors when you "blacked out" or could not remember what you did or lost track of time? If so, describe how you felt about it then, after you sobered up or began to remember, both then and now.

_____

_____

_____

_____

_____

What do you consider "normal use" of drugs and alcohol and normal in relationship to the behaviors - - how much, how often and why do you consider this "normal."

_____

_____

_____

_____

_____

Has there ever been a time when you were able to be more in control of your alcohol / drug use / behaviors or perhaps even quit all together? Describe in your own words when this happened, how many times, if more than once, and why you think it was possible.

What motivated you to try and what degree of success did you experience?

_____

_____

_____

_____

_____

In your own words, explain your pattern of thinking in the past year, how often do you thoughts focus on using alcohol and drugs or the behaviors – both now and your past activity and thinking.

_____

_____

_____

_____

_____

Try to estimate how frequently and how intensely those thoughts have been prevalent and have interrupted what you were thinking at that time, even if those interruptions have been minor or short-lived.

_____

_____

_____

_____

_____

Describe how often and in what way your "normal life" patterns were interrupted or interfered with by the use of drugs/alcohol/the behaviors.

_____

_____

_____

_____

_____

What responsibilities or obligations were set aside when this happened?

_____

_____

_____

_____

_____

How much of your daily/weekly/monthly time was spent on either using drugs/alcohol or participating in the behaviors, seeking or recovering from the effects?

_____

_____

_____

_____

_____

After completing the writing, lay it all aside and think through your responses. Are they complete and as accurate as possible? Are they open, honest and transparent? Do the things you have written reflect your true heart and emotions? Pray and ask God to show you what you will not admit to yourself or what the enemy of your soul, Satan, has blocked out or caused you to be ashamed of. Make the same request of Him that David did all those years ago when he struggled with sin and behaviors that were not pleasing to God.

"Search me, O God, and know my heart; Try me and know my anxious thoughts; And see if there be any hurtful way in me, And lead me in the everlasting way." Psalm 139:23 – 24 (NASB)

After spending that time in prayer, review all that you have written and make any changes or additions you think the Lord prompted or brought to mind. This is an important first step in accepting all the freedom and new life God has planned for you during your journey. When finished, pray and ask God with whom and how much He would want you to share of what you have written.

"I, the LORD, search the heart, I test the mind, Even to give to each man according to his ways, according to the results of his deeds." Jeremiah 17:10 (NASB)

Daniel L. Taylor

Stumbling blocks the enemy uses

Even when we sense the Lord asking us to be vulnerable and open, sharing our issues and needs with another, Satan can cause us to "shrink back" by lying to us. Satan and his demons will plant thoughts in our minds and hearts, such as – "You will be thought less of if you share that" or "No one will even be willing to work with you if you let them know that," or "God will condemn you if that ever gets known." All lies! All from the enemy who wants to keep you imprisoned! Remember who has the most compassionate heart: God!

"You, in Your great compassion, Did not forsake them in the wilderness; The pillar of cloud did not leave them by day, To guide them on their way, Nor the pillar of fire by night, to light for them the way in which they were to go. You gave Your good Spirit to instruct them, . . ." Nehemiah 9:19 – 20(a) (NASB)

Remember also who is the enemy of your soul? Satan and his demonic forces want nothing but harm for you now and for eternity! Jesus made sure everyone knew it!

"I am the door; if anyone enters through Me, he will be saved, and will go in and out and find pasture. The thief comes only to steal and kill and destroy; I came that they may have life, and have it abundantly. John 10:9 & 10 (NASB)

One of the most important facts that you should hold onto dearly at this stage of your journey is that change is not only possible, but also worth the pain you may be feeling. God's desire for all of His people, everyone who has been born, is to be transformed and live the way He designed us.

"He has regarded the prayer of the destitute and has not despised their prayer. This will be written for the generation to come, that a people yet to be created may praise the LORD. For He looked down from His holy height; From heaven the LORD gazed upon the earth, To hear the groaning of the prisoner, To set free those who were doomed to death" Psalm 102:17 – 20 (NASB)

The primary principle behind all that you will encounter and all the freedom you gain will be that you will be making an exchange. You can exchange the false beliefs about yourself, your world and your relationships for the truth of God. Addiction begins in an attempt to cope with life's issues by medicating ourselves to dampen the impact of believing falsely.

Once those lies take over our thinking, we seldom change unless we think differently. This journey is just that simple – we need to change the way we think!

"And do not be conformed to this world, but be transformed by the renewing of your mind, so that you may prove what the will of God is, that which is good and acceptable and perfect." *Romans 12:2 (NASB)*

Once you begin to think differently, the foundation of what guides your thinking becomes as important as your willingness to change. The word of God is the "mirror" that will reflect who God says you are in contrast to who you think you are. The truth must be primary in all you say, do and think.

"If you continue in My word, then you are truly disciples of Mine; and you will know the truth, and the truth will make you free." John 8:31b & 32(NASB)

Now take some time to lay aside your last writing, pray and rethink what you have written. After a time of reflecting and rethinking, then pray again, asking the Holy Spirit to reveal to you anything needed for this journey in knowing God's truth.

Be controlled by truth not emotions

After praying and thinking through what you wrote the first time and the changes you felt needed to be made, spend a few minutes writing about how you feel. What emotions have you experienced in the season of examining the fruit, or results of your past choices?

_____

_____

_____

_____

_____

When you look at your final draft, are you sad, angry, depressed, confused, etc?

_____

_____

_____

_____

_____

Who did you decide to share it with and how do you feel about sharing it with them?

_____

_____

_____

_____

_____

The evaluation of the Impact of the Past

The fruits of past choices

"So every good tree bears good fruit, but the bad tree bears bad fruit. A good tree cannot produce bad fruit, nor can a bad tree produce good fruit. Matthew 7:17 & 18 (NASB)

Addictions come in many forms, and their afflictions present themselves in many ways; addiction to heroin, alcohol, methamphetamine or any drug, an addiction to pornography or the Internet, an addiction to shopping or spending money; an addiction to same-sex relationships or adulterous relationships. While on this journey toward total freedom from addictions everyone should be aware of one of the simplest yet most profound principles found in God's word: all of these addictions are simply sin. According to the word of God, theft and the killing of another human being are viewed the same. It is all disobedience to God and it is sin, the result of sin is disastrous to life, family, society and our relationships with the holy and righteous God.

"Therefore what benefit were you then deriving from the things of which you are now ashamed? For the outcome of those things is death. But now having been freed from sin and in slave to God, you drive your benefit resulting in sanctification, and the outcome, eternal life. For the wages of sin is death, but the free gift of God is eternal life in Christ Jesus our Lord"
(Romans 6:21 – 23 (NASB)

Think back at your past and the relationships of your past. Many, if not most people imprisoned with addictions, damaged if not significantly destroyed many relationships that were productive and good. The relationships that were intact to some degree were those with individuals or groups of people who would agree with your addictions, or at least not raise strong objections to your addictions. Does that generally describe you? How have those even unhealthy relationships faired now that you have decided to break free and get help from the Lord?

Set aside some time right now and make note of the condition of the relationships you have had in the past 12 months before seeking help. Be honest and open with yourself!

_____

_____

_____

_____

_____

Set this aside now and continue reading, but at the end of this section, come back to these notes and re-think what you have written and, after careful consideration, pray. Ask God to show what He thinks is most important for you to do about those relationships after you finish the changes He is prompting you to make in your life. Don't act on those until after you have completed this journey, but return to these notes occasionally throughout this journey and add or modify what the Holy Spirit prompts you to do.

Some Challenges to face

Your journey into freedom can be one of great rewards and big changes in life and can result in the peace desired and sought after by every human who has ever lived. But with great reward can also come one of the most challenging journeys ever undertaken. At times, the trail may seem as though you are traveling great distances with no prior conditioning or practice. You may be out of your comfort zone and feel as if you are walking alone. You will experience seasons with varied emotions and thoughts; one day you will feel great joy in your journey and the next you could feel the current journey is worse than the addiction itself. One challenge to change may be just that, your feelings. The entire spectrum of emotions and feelings will course through your mind and thoughts, sometimes changing from one to the other or more rapidly than you ever imagined possible.

However, with all challenges and joys, you must keep your primary focus on the fact that Satan does not want you to succeed.

"The thief comes only to steal and kill and destroy..." John 10:10 (NASB)

You are facing a season of opportunity, and those around you will be watching your actions, words, and decisions with a great deal of interest, hoping that you will finally find freedom from addictions. Keep in mind, however, that those around you may not be as willing to believe that you are truly going to make a change this time. It goes back to the old saying "shame on you if you fool me once, shame on me if you fool me twice." How can success be accomplished? Who can help walk through this season of change alongside you? Knowing that God brought you into this journey and has provided you with a "new start" – "fresh start" - - should be an encouragement for you. He has known the dark times in your life and knows you truly want to be freed from this prison, which should be even more of an encouragement for you.

He will then provide you with the right relationship opportunities. That very important first relationship must be with Jesus Christ, God's own Son, as Lord and Savior. If you have never asked Jesus into your life, now is that time. Without Him being Lord, Savior and the most important relationship you have, all that you will encounter during this time will be "hollow" and without any real power to make the changes needed. Many have gone before you in trying to get free from addictions, some much worse than yours, and those around them watched in hope, yet were ultimately disappointed because of their failures. The Holy Spirit is Who prompts us to accept Jesus and is prompting you now. What will you do?

"Therefore, since we have so great a cloud of witnesses surrounding us, let us also lay aside every encumbrance and the sin which so easily entangles us, and let us run with endurance the race that is set before us, fixing our eyes on Jesus, the author and perfecter of faith, who for the joy set before Him endured the cross," Hebrews 12:1&2a (NASB)

Get ahead of some challenges **now**!!!

It is as simple as believing these words and repeating them as if you were standing with Jesus in front of you right now – consider praying these principles in your own words right now – *"God, I know I have been wrong and done things that are not acceptable to you – I have sinned – I believe Jesus was born, walked this earth in human form and is you Son. I believe He was tortured, killed and rose from the dead and now sits beside you in heaven.*

Even though I don't understand much about that, I believe it is true. I also want to ask you to forgive all the things I have done that you are not pleased with and walk with me from now on.

I ask these things, because I want a relationship with You now and for eternity. I pray these words in the name of Your Son, Jesus"

Welcome to God's family

If this is your first time praying that way, welcome into the best family in the world, the family of Jesus. If you have prayed that prayer before but simply drifted off course, welcome back into the family of God. Now it is time to exercise the power available to all who believe and wish to deepen their relationship with Jesus. He will walk through this journey with you and so will others who know and love Him. One of the keys to freedom in any type of addiction is having another walk alongside you while you learn how to trust you own decision making and choices.

The second most important part of true change is having others walk this journey out alongside you in truth, honesty, and transparency. That sounds scary because it can be, after having lived under the control of an addiction and trying to keep many things hidden and undiscovered. Bringing hidden things into the light of day can be scary. Not everyone is the right person to share some of the hidden, embarrassing and, often times, shameful things with, but there is someone "assigned by God" for you. God knows who that person is and how much is right to share and when to share it with him or her. One thing for sure, since He already knows you deeply, Jesus is always the right One to share with!

Getting deeply involved with your local, evangelical Christian Church is extremely important. Staying involved and finding who God has planned to be a part of your life provides many benefits, critical to success in the freedom you want and need. God designed humans to be in relationship with Him and one another. True transparent relationships that are safe and good for healing are part of God's design and plan.

"Therefore, brethren, since we have confidence to enter the holy place by the blood of Jesus, by a new and living way which He inaugurated for us through the veil, that is, His flesh, and since we have a great priest over the house of God, let us draw near with a sincere heart in full assurance of faith, having our hearts sprinkled clean from an evil conscience and our bodies washed with pure water. Let us hold fast the confession of our hope without wavering, for He who promised is faithful; and let us consider how to stimulate one another to love and good deeds, not forsaking our own assembling together, as is the habit of some, but encouraging one another; and all the more as you see the day drawing near. Hebrews 10:19 – 25 (NASB)

Be on guard

When you find a degree of freedom from the addiction that has imprisoned you in the past, you must be careful in many areas of life. One of the most important things to take care about is not substituting one addiction for another. In many of the world's programs for addictions, people transfer their addiction from what used to be controlling them to a seemingly good thing and never find true liberty and freedom. That can easily happen when that good thing is a meeting that seems to support abstinence from the substance or behavior, but promotes the meeting itself or the group as the path to continued freedom. In effect what happens is that meeting or group want to be the substitute for God, that is from Satan. God did not design us that way. He designed us to live free from all things that draw us away from Him being our source of strength and power to overcome the sin.

"Submit therefore to God. Resist the devil and he will flee from you. Draw near to God and He will draw near to you" James 4:7 & 8 (NASB)

God has designed His people to help the world around them in many ways. The most important way is to know and love Him above all else. He also knew how difficult that would be after the very first of His creation, Adam and Eve, disobeyed His design for them and their relationship with Him.

The second purpose in His design for us is to help one another when things became tough. He does not want man to be alone and, even after giving Eve to Adam, He instructed them to have children and grow as a family. That family growth and eventually extended family had at the core the principle of helping one another and loving one another. He promised them many things if they lived within that design and purpose as well as promising them He would also be there for them when they obeyed His ways.

"For I will set My eyes on them for good, and I will bring them again to this land; and I will build them up and not overthrow them, and I will plant them and not pluck them up. 'I will give them a heart to know Me, for I am the LORD; and they will be My people, and I will be their God, for they will return to Me with their whole heart." Jeremiah 24:6-7 (NASB)

How well you succeed in gaining and keeping your freedom is based on one simple principle: finding and keeping a good, healthy and productive relationship with many in God's family. Even when the old, healthy relationships are damaged or destroyed, God will make a way to restore them while He gives you good gifts in other relationships.

I can nearly hear your thoughts as you read these lines – "Won't I get dependent upon those relationships also, the way I was warned about the other groups and meetings?" The answer to that concern is important for everyone involved in every relationship – "It can become that way if you or the group or meeting people are not careful." One of the principles that makes these "faith-centered" relationships different is the group and individuals priorities. If they are focused on God's word and His warnings, they will always point everyone toward God and their relationship with Jesus Christ as their most important priority.

Is that always true – remember, every human who is alive or ever has been alive, except Jesus, is prone to selfishness and must fight that tendency hard. Keeping yourself and others focused on Jesus is always an important ministry we all have toward one another.

"Therefore, since we have so great a cloud of witnesses surrounding us, let us also lay aside every encumbrance and the sin which so easily entangles us, and let us run with endurance the race that is set before us, fixing our eyes on Jesus, the author and perfecter of faith," Hebrews 12:1 & 2a (NASB)

The value of these good, healthy Christian relationships cannot be overstated. Once you made the decision to seek freedom from addictions and separated yourself from that lifestyle and, hopefully put distance between you and the relationships involved in your addiction, you are or will begin to feel alone.

Don't move ahead, just move on

Loneliness and isolation take a toll on everyone who finds themselves in that situation. The toll can only be "paid" in two basic ways – find an old friend or make new ones. The old friends, both in people and the "old pal" of addictive actions, will only get seven times worse if you go back to them. God knew that and warns us.

"When the unclean spirit goes out of a man, it passes through waterless places seeking rest, and not finding any, it says, 'I will return to my house from which I came'. And when it comes, it finds it swept and put in order. Then it goes and takes along seven other spirits more evil than itself, and they go in and live there; and the last state of that man becomes worse than the first." Luke 11:24 – 26 (NASB)

Pray – step back – review and think

The only true means you have is to "pray" as you continue to seek more freedom and develop more productive relationships. It is critical to your present progress and your future freedom to find one or two good, healthy Christian friends to walk the journey with you. Take some time now to set aside your journey and the progress you have made so far through this material and review the questions and the responses that you have written. Go all the way to the very beginning and review all the questions and your answers in the order they were asked.

But before you do that, two important things need to happen – Get a notebook or a few sheets of paper and a pencil or pen – then pray and ask God to open your heart and eyes to see what He wants you to see. In that prayer, tell Him what you are doing, even though He knows.

Something as simple as this statement – *"Lord, I want to see with my heart and eyes what you see with yours, but I have a pencil and paper ready Lord, it is so important to me to hear what you have to say, I am ready to write it down. Lord I also know that Satan will try to trick me, so I ask you to bind him from my life today and forever more, with the blood of Jesus and because of the power of Jesus victory over him, in Jesus name"*

Now that you have done that and, hopefully, heard from the Holy Spirit about who to ask to walk with you in this journey, you should understand why new Christian friends and the Church body is so important. When anyone is on the receiving end of help, some important thoughts and principles come into play. Some who receive the type of help you are receiving will begin to "settle in" and become very comfortable in being on the receiving side of the relationship. That is not always a bad thing *for a short season*. The more comfortable you become with your new relationships the more willing to be open you will be in the future. As you grow in this openness with another who wants you to be successful, the more freedom you will find in sharing your struggles with God and others, which disarms the enemy of your soul.

Caution

The danger lies in growing so comfortable simply from receiving life giving advice and encouragement from others that you develop the mindset of being entitled to receive from others. Once that takes hold, you begin to feel no obligation or even desire to give back in any way. That may not seem like it would be something that is a part of your personality, but it is a part of everyone of mankind. Once that gets to be a pattern it can be very damaging and cripple your future progress as well as your current search for freedom.

That applies within the individual, one-on-one relationships as well as in the corporate relationship with the entire Church body locally. That pattern of thinking has even been known to corrupt the perspective on the greater universal church. Caution should be exercised by you in this area. Even though receiving life giving advice and help is good and acceptable in God's eyes, being dependent upon it can be very damaging!

"All things are lawful for me, but not all things are profitable. All things are lawful for me, but I will not be mastered by anything." 1 Corinthians 6:12 (NASB)

Another element of establishing and building strong relationships with one or two individuals that is important is the healing that often results from the time together. Getting another believer's perspective on what has happened to us and how we view those events in contrast to the way God would have us view them can be very healing.

There are events in nearly everyone's past that has created a wound, sometimes in significant ways. The good thing is God has planned for his people a way to overcome those past wounds and hurts. Sometimes people come from families or have had close friendships that did not wound you outwardly, but they withheld the love and acceptance that we all need. Another possibility from our past that is more prominent than expected is the terrible things that people do to one another in families and close, supposedly safe, relationships. It is often very traumatic to us and affects our image of God. You could have experienced some of this in your past. Uncovering and healing from these could be the key to your freedom from the controlling addiction you are looking to be free from.

What is important for you to know is that it is certainly the key to remaining free in the future. Your success can be negatively impacted if these things are kept beneath the surface and allowed to fester.

"Everyone who comes to Me and hears My words and acts on them, I will show you whom he is like: he is like a man building a house, who dug deep and laid a foundation on the rock; and when a flood occurred, the torrent burst against that house and could not shake it, because it had been well built. But the one who has heard and has not acted accordingly, is like a man who built a house on the ground without any foundation; and the torrent burst against it and immediately it collapsed, and the ruin of that house was great." Luke 6:47 – 49 (NASB)

All of us must be very careful to build on the solid foundation of being healed by God from all aspects of our wounds that come from the past experiences.

"Brethren, I do not regard myself as having laid hold of it yet; but one thing I do: forgetting what lies behind and reaching forward to what lies ahead.. " Philippians 3:13 (NASB)

Take a few minutes now and lay aside the reading once more and pray. Ask God to show you those past relationships that have hurt your heart and soul and have become imbedded in your thoughts. Remember the same principle applies every time you pray about throughout this entire journey. Let Him know you have a pencil and paper ready because you desire to hear and remember what He has to say to you!

Now, write a paragraph or more on each relationship that you have in your past and perhaps even the relationships you have been in or are still in today, that have hurt you. Be sure to write down what happened and how you feel about what happened. Let your true emotions come flowing out of your heart and onto the paper. Holding back will erode away your "solid foundation," and when things get tough the torrent will cause your freedom to collapse.

You may need more room than is provided below. Feel free to add what you need to let as much as possible to come flowing out now!

_____

_____

_____

Daniel L. Taylor

_____
_____
_____
_____
_____
_____
_____
_____
_____
_____
_____
_____
_____
_____
_____
_____
_____

Now that you have taken time to pray and write down those relationships that need healing, share what you have written with someone more spiritually mature than you. Don't worry, it is safe and will be held in confidence. God has designed the relationships in His people in such a way as to help each other get past the things that hold them back from maturing in our journey. He loves us and wants the best for us. In later segments more will be explained about how the relationships with the larger body of Christ will be helpful and healing in nature. Hopefully, you will have gained a deeper level of trust in what God has planned for you in this journey.

When the gardener experiences the first segment of the winter months, he looks back on what went wrong and how those things can be made right for the next season. The gardener wants good results, and after examining what went wrong last season, he next turns his thoughts and focus on what mistakes he may have made.

In this next season of change for you, we'll have you seriously look and think about what your own personal responsibilities might be. This happens only after you have identified and agreed with one or two Christians that God has brought into your path to walk together through this journey.

Be aware of the old tricks

For now, look at the following from Genesis and the fall of mankind into sin and study the situation, looking for clues that help us understand why problems arise on our lives. Look closely at the dialogue between Eve and Satan and try to uncover a few tricks Satan used and still uses today. With this study you will gain some tips about how Satan may try to trick you.

Begin with God's simple instruction in *Genesis 2:15 - 17 (NASB)* to Adam –

"Then the LORD God took the man and put him into the garden of Eden to cultivate it and keep it. The LORD God commanded the man, saying, "From any tree of the garden you may eat freely; but from the tree of the knowledge of good and evil you shall not eat, for in the day that you eat from it you will surely die."

Your opinion will be asked in this section. Do not be afraid of being off track; nearly everyone is in these situations. What this journey is about is finding the truth of God every time, not being right all the time.

What is the most difficult thing, ***in your opinion***, about listening to God's instruction here and actually following through?

_____

_____

_____

_____

_____

_____

_____

_____

_____

_____

Now take a look at the details of the fall.

"Now the serpent was more crafty than any beast of the field which the LORD God had made. And he said to the woman, "Indeed, has God said, 'You shall not eat from any tree of the garden'?" The woman said to the serpent, "From the fruit of the trees of the garden

we may eat ³but from the fruit of the tree which is in the middle of the garden, God has said, 'You shall not eat from it or touch it, or you will die.'" The serpent said to the woman, "You surely will not die! "For God knows that in the day you eat from it your eyes will be opened, and you will be like God, knowing good and evil." When the woman saw that the tree was good for food, and that it was a delight to the eyes, and that the tree was desirable to make one wise, she took from its fruit and ate; and she gave also to her husband with her, and he ate. Then the eyes of both of them were opened, and they knew that they were naked; and they sewed fig leaves together and made themselves loin coverings.

They heard the sound of the LORD God walking in the garden in the cool of the day, and the man and his wife hid themselves from the presence of the LORD God among the trees of the garden. Then the LORD God called to the man, and said to him, "Where are you?" He said, "I heard the sound of You in the garden, and I was afraid because I was naked; so I hid myself." And He said, "Who told you that you were naked? Have you eaten from the tree of which I commanded you not to eat?" The man said, "The woman whom You gave to be with me, she gave me from the tree, and I ate." Then the LORD God said to the woman, "What is this you have done?" And the woman said, "The serpent deceived me, and I ate."
Genesis 3:1 – 13 (NASB)

Write out what you see happening and how that impacted mankind from then until now. Personalize it to yourself and how these clues can show you what Satan will try to get you to believe about yourself and God. ***Remember, your opinion matters and there is no wrong opinion for you to have at this time.***

_____

_____

_____

_____

_____

_____

_____

_____

_____

_____

_____

The Past is past but what can I learn

Why and how did this happen

Often the things of the past get blurry and the details are hard to remember. Our own imaginations, as well as the busyness of life in general, can add to the blurriness. When you think about the impact of addictions on your body and, in particular, your brain chemistry, it is a wonder that anything can be recalled with any clarity.

Nutritional compromise resulting from addictions to chemicals and behaviors is a scientific fact. Scientifically measurable damage in some cases and the full impact of the nutritional deficits on behaviors and thinking patterns is still being researched. What is known about the impact can help you understand why your life became so "out of control" and you were not able to "simply stop," as many may have suggested to you was possible. Even after you study and understand the physical impact of your addiction, you will see clearly that apart from the help of God, it would not have been possible. Repairing the damage done to your body will also only be possible with God's help and guidance. Listen to what Jesus says about the impossibility of man to solve his problems and the power of God that makes all things possible.

"But He said, "The things that are impossible with people are possible with God." Luke 18:27 (NASB)

Think back when you first started coping with life through your addiction. There were likely times when you could stop for a period of time rather easily.

Taking a break from the addiction for a "season," however long that may have been, is not all that difficult for some people, maybe even you. What happened to those times when I could "take a break," you may be asking yourself? One simple phrase that best describes what happened and why it was difficult to stop completely comes to mind: "hijacked brain".

Chemical shifts in the brain often begin with the first manifestation of the addictive behavior or substance use. Even addictions that do not involve chemicals can alter brain chemistry almost from the beginning. Shopping addictions, eating disorders, addiction to pornography, internet use addictions, sexual addiction of any type, and many other addictions that do not involve drugs or alcohol begin to shift the balance of chemicals in the brain.

Reversing change – eliminating shame

Those shifting brain chemistry balances are not an excuse for continuing with the addiction and acting in ways that the Lord does not approve. The chemical changes are important to understand so that you can grasp a way to regain control in the future, should something arise that brings that coping choice into consideration. Brain chemistry is one of many factors that steals from you your power to quit. Ultimately you are responsible for beginning to cope with life's stresses by beginning it in the first place. The term *"seemingly powerless"* is used so you can understand there was and still is another way to regain control over your addiction. Sounds simple, and it truly is simple when you have a better understanding of life and God's design for living.

Before providing that knowledge, you need to read and pray and try to understand what God has to say about you and your circumstances. What we believe about ourselves is often flawed and, in some cases, simply a lie. What God wants us to trust in is Him and His word, using it as the mirror for our lives. The word of God reflects how God sees us, and He sent His Son, Jesus to reconcile all things to Himself. Read these scriptures, pray, asking the Holy Spirit to help you understand how important these words are and how critical they are to your future. These are Jesus' actual words for us to understand where we find our security

"If a kingdom is divided against itself, that kingdom cannot stand. If a house is divided against itself, that house will not be able to stand. If Satan has risen up against himself and is divided, he cannot stand, but he is finished! But no one can enter the strong man's house and plunder his property unless he first binds the strong man, and then he will plunder his

house. Truly I say to you, all sins shall be forgiven the sons of men . . . ", Mark 3:24 – 28a (NASB)

He understands our divided thinking about all things in life. He truly wants us to understand that He knows our struggles against the enemy. Jesus walked as a fully human being on this earth and can relate to all we are encountering and will encounter. God has dealt with these types of issues throughout all of history. He knows what we need!

"For I know the plans that I have for you,' declares the LORD, 'plans for welfare and not for calamity to give you a future and a hope. 'Then you will call upon Me and come and pray to Me, and I will listen to you. You will seek Me and find Me when you search for Me with all your heart. I will be found by you,' declares the LORD . ." Jeremiah 29:11 – 14a (NASB)

His plans are for your success and well being, according to His designs for your life. He wants us all to know, when we find ourselves in a difficult situation or making a choice that will impact our future, He is there for us. He also wants us to understand that when we turn to Him and His ways, we can win the battles we face daily. We can do more than simply win, thanks to His word as our mirror, which reflects who we truly are in His eyes.

"What then shall we say to these things? If God is for us, who is against us, He who did not spare His own Son, but delivered Him over for us all, how will He not also with Him freely give us all things? Who will bring a charge against God's elect? God is the one who justifies; who is the one who condemns? Christ Jesus is He who died, yes, rather who was raised, who is at the right hand of God, who also intercedes for us. Who will separate us from the love of Christ? Will tribulation, or distress, or persecution, or famine, or nakedness, or peril, or sword? Just as it is written, "FOR YOUR SAKE WE ARE BEING PUT TO DEATH ALL DAY LONG; WE WERE CONSIDERED AS SHEEP TO BE SLAUGHTERED." But in all these things we overwhelmingly conquer through Him who loved us. For I am convinced that neither death, nor life, nor angels, nor principalities, nor things present, nor things to come, nor powers, nor height, nor depth, nor any other created thing, will be able to separate us from the love of God, which is in Christ Jesus our Lord."
Romans 8:31 – 37 (NASB)

God truly sees you and all of those who believe in Jesus as being able to win the battles, become conquerors and live a life of victory over our own battles in our thoughts and decisions and against the enemy.

Daniel L. Taylor

One of the most encouraging truths about Jesus, in addition to spending eternity with Him and Father God, comes from what He spoke to those who had followed Him while He was on earth.

"Truly, truly, I say to you, he who believes in Me, the works that I do, he will do also; and greater works than these he will do; because I go to the Father. Whatever you ask in My name, that will I do, so that the Father may be glorified in the Son. If you ask Me anything in My name, I will do it". John 12:12 – 14 (NASB)

The words of Jesus in these verses must become much more than just encouragement for you as you journey from the bondage of addiction into the freedom God has waiting for you. Whereas at times the battle may seem more than you can stand, the life of freedom is more than you can imagine. If every person who has ever been imprisoned by addictions or the consequences of bad relationships, both in their physical being and thinking patterns, who has been set free through God's power could speak with one voice, they would tell you it is worth the fight ahead.

The enemy of your soul wants to bring fear and doubt into your mind. That is normal and a good indicator that God has some great things ahead for you. If you write those fears and doubts down, share them with the person you have chosen as a partner in this journey, the enemy can be defeated more easily.

"Submit therefore to God. Resist the devil and he will flee from you. Draw near to God and He will draw near to you. Cleanse your hands, you sinners; and purify your hearts, you double-minded." James 4:7 – 8 (NASB)

Take a few minutes right now and write out the most troubling doubt you have. After writing your most troubling doubt, take a few minutes and write down your greatest fears.
The doubts that trouble me the most are:

_____

_____

_____

_____

_____

_____

_____

_____

_____

_____

My greatest fear is:

_____

_____

_____

_____

_____

_____

_____

_____

_____

_____

_____

_____

_____

_____

The Bible is the mirror through which we see what God has to say about us. He also knows all that we are facing and all that we will face and how we feel about those things. Feelings should never dictate what we believe, yet God knows they have an impact on us. In the Bible, God tells is more than 365 times to "***fear not***" or "***do not be afraid***". There are 365 days in each year, and it is no coincidence that God encouraged us more than 365 times this way.

Before you try to understand the various scientific information regarding the nutritional consequences of your past, you need to better understand the Biblical differences between body, soul, and spirit.

What comprises the body is somewhat obvious: skin, internal organs (heart in this context is the pump that circulates blood) brain (in this context it is the organ inside the skull and the associated neural pathways and nerves), muscles, and the rest of what you can see or can be seen. Spiritually the "flesh" is not the outer portion of the skin, it is the desires that most have trouble with trying to do what is not pleasing to God.

Daniel L. Taylor

What comprises the soul is a little less easily understood and more complex. The soul is best described as the will (what you set your mind on doing or having, the determination you exercise when something is important to you), the past memories of your experiences, both pleasurable and painful in nature and your old thinking patterns that draw you away from God. The soul is the battleground the enemy fights to win control of and what will be perfected when a believer dies. The soul is what the Holy Spirit is trying to train in "Godliness" by bringing conviction of the wrongs you do, when you know what God expects and you do otherwise.

The spirit, once you believe in Jesus, is perfect because the Lord enters in and resides. The Holy Spirit resides in all believers' hearts and fights against the old ways and old memories that reside in your soul. The spirit of your old man has been changed and a new spirit has been given to you, even when you do not sense it in a real way.

"One of the scribes came and heard them arguing, and recognizing that He had answered them well, asked Him, "What commandment is the foremost of all?" Jesus answered, "The foremost is, 'HEAR, O ISRAEL! THE LORD OUR GOD IS ONE LORD; AND YOU SHALL LOVE THE LORD YOUR GOD WITH ALL YOUR HEART, AND WITH ALL YOUR SOUL, AND WITH ALL YOUR MIND, AND WITH ALL YOUR STRENGTH.' "The second is this, 'YOU SHALL LOVE YOUR NEIGHBOR AS YOURSELF.' There is no other commandment greater than these.""Mark 12:28 – 31 (NASB)

What God expects us to do is to grow in our love for Him in all areas of our lives. That will result in His being pleased with us and our actions. Since the body is the temple of the Lords, He wants us to take care of it and understand what our responsibility is in repairing the damage addiction has caused. Throughout this next section you will see definitions which will be helpful in understanding how science and God work together to repair the damage of addiction.

God – science- the body

The *American Dietetic Association (ADA)* has officially recognized that, "Many debilitating nutritional consequences result from drug and alcohol abuse. Chronic nutrition impairment causes serious damage to the liver and brain, which reinforces the craving for more drugs and alcohol and perpetuates the *psychological aspect* of addiction."

"Psychological aspects" are defined by Webster's dictionary as:" *relating to, characteristic of, directed toward, influencing, arising in, or acting through the mind especially in its affective or cognitive functions <the* psychological *aspects of a problem> or : directed toward the will or toward the mind specifically in its cognitive function"*

Furthermore, the ADA suggests, "Nutrition makes a difference in the rate and quality of physical recovery, which prepares individuals to function at a higher level cognitively, mentally, and socially."

Research indicates that a primary reason for high success or high failure rates in any type of treatment environment can be directly related to the surroundings in which the treatment occurs. Developing new living habits during treatment, coupled with the strong support system in a Godly environment where Godly principles are taught is critical to successful outcomes. Healthy, God designed health practices in exercise, proper nutritional practices, and proper balance in work and rest must be put into place. Successful treatment and healing from the former life controlled by addictions must involve healing and restoration of the body and brain. **Diet and nutrition play key roles in that process as well as in healthy living in true Godly obedience, no matter the subject!**

"God blessed them; and God said to them, "Be fruitful and multiply, and fill the earth, and subdue it; and rule over the fish of the sea and over the birds of the sky and over every living thing that moves on the earth." Then God said, "Behold, I have given you every plant yielding seed that is on the surface of all the earth, and every tree which has fruit yielding seed; it shall be food for you; and to every beast of the earth and to every bird of the sky and to ever thing that moves on the earth which has life, I have given every green plant for food"; and it was so. Genesis 1:28-30 (NASB)

Ongoing Godly nutritional practices are critical in order to achieve real and lasting recovery from any addiction. Of those studied who have stayed alcohol and drug-free for substantial periods of time, proper health practices and remaining faithful to prayer and the Word of God are some of the most common elements in their changed lives.

Whenever anyone lives according to their own designs and make choices and determinations outside of God's plan for their lives - - such as turning to addictions as a way of coping with the stress is of life - - significant damage is done to their bodies and souls. In an effort to restore mankind to his favor, God gave a message to his servant Ezekiel. God speaks of a constant supply of fresh water coming straight from his provision and of the kind of nutrition that would heal the people.

"the river on its bank, on one side and on the other, will grow all kinds of trees for food. Their leaves will not wither and their fruit will not fail. They will bear every month because their water flows from the sanctuary, and their fruit will be for food and their leaves for healing." Ezekiel 47:12 (NASB)

That same healing is available for us today if we live according to God's design!

Many persons simply do not eat enough food or the right foods when they are preoccupied with their addiction, which was most likely the same with you. When they did eat, the addiction, especially to substances, kept the body from properly absorbing and breaking down nutrients and expelling toxins.

In one clinical study, more than three-quarters of people being treated for addictions were classified as having unsatisfactory nutritional states, with malnutrition a distinct possibility. They were typically deficient in a number of vitamins, minerals, proteins, and fatty acids. Addictive substances affect food and liquid intake, taste preference, and body weight. Opioids can alter cholesterol, calcium, and potassium levels. Potassium is especially important because an imbalance in this electrolyte can influence cardiac problems.

Nutritional supplements – e.g., - vitamins, amino acids, herbal products – and other nutrients are believed capable of restoring proper balance in the brain. Also, eliminating or reducing certain substances (sugars, simple starches, caffeine) and increasing protein intake may help rebalance brain chemistry. All this in conjunction with eating properly, abstaining from substance use and abuse, along with a strong faith in the "Healing GOD" will restore an individual to wholeness.

During the first two years of recovery, improved nutrition also can help heal physical damage to the body caused by nutrient depletion. Nutrition cannot be neglected by anyone desiring to be released from the addictive lifestyle, renewed in their hope of a bright and blessed future and restored to wholeness.

Addictions to behaviors that are displeasing to God have similar correlations to the damage done by ingesting substances. All sin is damaging, especially when that sin begins to become your god.

". . . and do not go after other gods to serve them and to worship them, and do not provoke Me to anger with the work of your hands, and I will do you no harm. . ." Jeremiah 25:6 (NASB)

During the early stages of the process of turning away from the former life and turning toward a life free from substance abuse, you must be cautious not simply to substitute one addiction for another. Many who stayed alcohol and drug free yet remain in the same pattern of thinking substitute large-scale use of coffee, sugar, and cigarettes for the formerly used drugs. The cornerstone of freedom from all addiction is Godly balance in all things, especially in repairing the damage done to your body.

The concept of healthy eating coupled with exercise and Godly living is to do all things within your power to strengthen your metabolism, increase your energy level, and increase your awareness of well-being. Patience is a virtue in this process. The damage done was done over time, a great deal of time - - the repair process takes time also!

One of the life-long practices that lead to healthy living is a critical practice in early stages of repairing the damage from addictions – drinking six to eight large glasses of water each day. Increasing the amount of water ingested daily, in most cases, is even better. Just like the plants spoken of in the verse quoted earlier, the "water flowing from the throne" causes the human body to be more productive.

"The river on its bank, on one side and on the other, will grow all kinds of trees for food. Their leaves will not wither and their fruit will not fail. They will bear every month because their water flows from the sanctuary, and their fruit will be for food and their leaves for healing." Ezekiel 47:12 (NASB)

Recovery is much more than simply stopping the use of the active substances and behaviors, as many wise and highly educated people may think. God's wisdom cautions us about our own wisdom.

"Do not be wise in your own eyes; Fear the LORD and turn away from evil. It will be healing to your body and refreshment to your bones." Proverbs 3:7- 8 (NASB)

Even the moods you will encounter in the process of being set free from the prison of addictions will be somewhat improved by proper nutritional practices. You need to be very cautious about allowing emotions to control your thinking and behaviors. Emotions are not bad, but being controlled by your emotions is the reverse of the way God designed you. He has given you emotions to express your true heart, not to define truth. That will be addressed later, but for now, look at how what you eat can help monitor your mood.

Food-Mood Connections

Depression and other battles commonly fought by people imprisoned by addictions can be at least partially attributed to poor nutrition. Hypoglycemia (low blood sugar) and potentially unidentified food allergies that have been created by living outside of the design of God can cause emotional mood problems. The battle is truly won by your trust in God's healing power. As you live according to His design for your life, the physical and emotional conditions improve you become aware and practice good nutrition and regular exercise.

When you have a stable emotional condition and are not "ruled and controlled" by your emotions, you are more likely not to return to your former addiction. Not doing all you can spiritually and physically can make it nearly impossible to overcome a negative mood. Some of the most common emotional conditions that take control are anxiety and depression. For example, thiamin deficiency, common among some imprisoned by addictions, can lead to depression and irritability. Iron deficiency, frequently occurring in chemical addictions, can result in anemia, with symptoms such as lethargy and decreased mental function.

An important relationship between blood-sugar levels and mood is often emphasized in much secular literature. If you return to the old addictions, especially drug and alcohol use, it will cause blood glucose levels to peak and then dip rapidly, causing a series of mood swings.

Even moderate drops in your blood glucose level can cause irritability, and more rapid glucose cycling can cause severe aggression. Peaks and troughs can be a problem and are most often caused by diets rich in refined sugar (e.g., "junk foods"). This type of diet can negatively affect your mental performance and thinking patterns, even if you do not become hypoglycemic.

Deficiencies of nutrients such as B-complex vitamins and amino acids can have serious negative effects on your freedom and life in general. Certain amino acids are critical building blocks for your brain's neurotransmitters that regulate your mood and emotions.

For example, tryptophan is a precursor of serotonin, which is important in your fight against depression. Adequate amounts of vitamins B_3 and B_6 are needed to convert tryptophan to serotonin.

In God's world, balance and living according to His guidance in all areas of your life, nutritional supplements aren't needed in many cases, if not most. But the lack of wise living in accordance with God's design produces open doors for the enemy and results in mood swings in people with addictive behaviors and practices. Not eating properly or not eating at all, without God calling for the "fast," leads to sadness.

"A joyful heart makes a cheerful face, But when the heart is sad, the spirit is broken. The mind of the intelligent seeks knowledge, But the mouth of fools feeds on folly. All the days of the afflicted are bad, But a cheerful heart has a continual feast. Proverbs 15: 13-15(NASB

Maintaining a proper, positive upbeat attitude during the entire process of learning to live a life free from addictions and glorifying God should always be your first and most important priority! He will honor you when He is who and what is most important in your life and your transformation. He desires your full devotion to Him and His ways. You can then enjoy His favor when you give Him your undivided attention, and He will carry you through the prison doors and set you free.

Be aware

Being patient and understanding some important facts in the early stages of changing your eating habits is critical to your successful, life-long transformation. In the early stages of all aspects of your journey, especially your eating changes, you could actually feel worse rather than feel better. That is the period when the toxins are being flushed from your body. Those toxins have built up over time and take time to be flushed out of your cell structures.

Two very important scripture verses must become a part of your encouragement and your daily life in these early stages of your journey. Read them daily, meditate on them frequently, and pray. Ask your mentor on this journey to help you stay focused upon these principles.

"Only be strong and very courageous; be careful to do according to all the law which Moses My servant commanded you; do not turn from it to the right or to the left, so that you may have success wherever you go. "This book of the law shall not depart from your mouth, but you shall meditate on it day and night, so that you may be careful to do according to all that

Daniel L. Taylor

is written in it; for then you will make your way prosperous, and then you will have success. "Have I not commanded you? Be strong and courageous! Do not tremble or be dismayed, for the LORD your God is with you wherever you go." Joshua 1:7-9 (NASB)

"I waited patiently for the Lord; and He inclined unto me, and heard my cry. He also brought me up out of a horrible pit, out of the miry clay, and set my feet upon a rock, and established my steps. He has put a new song in my mouth -- praise to our God; many will see it and fear, and will trust in the Lord. Psalm 40:1 -3 (NASB)

The enemy will come after your thinking and your effort to become all that God has for you to be. This enemy is older than creation and uses some of the same tactics and methods against you as he has against all who choose to glorify God by being transformed. Take some time and write your thoughts and ideas down as to what this Psalm leads you to understand.

"O Lord, rebuke me not in Your wrath, And chasten me not in Your burning anger. For Your arrows have sunk deep into me, And Your hand has pressed down on me. There is no soundness in my flesh because of Your indignation; There is no health in my bones because of my sin. For my iniquities are gone over my head; As a heavy burden they weigh too much for me. My wounds grow foul and fester Because of my folly. I am bent over and greatly bowed down; I go mourning all day long. For my loins are filled with burning, And there is no soundness in my flesh. I am benumbed and badly crushed; I groan because of the agitation of my heart. Lord, all my desire is before You; And my sighing is not hidden from You. My heart throbs, my strength fails me; And the light of my eyes, even that has gone from me. My loved ones and my friends stand aloof from my plague; And my kinsmen stand afar off. Those who seek my life lay snares for me; And those who seek to injure me have threatened destruction, And they devise treachery all day long. But I, like a deaf man, do not hear; And I am like a mute man who does not open his mouth.

Yes, I am like a man who does not hear, And in whose mouth are no arguments. For I hope in You, O LORD; You will answer, O Lord my God. For I said, "May they not rejoice over me, Who, when my foot slips, would magnify themselves against me." For I am ready to fall, And my sorrow is continually before me. For I confess my iniquity; I am full of anxiety because of my sin. But my enemies are vigorous and strong, And many are those who hate me wrongfully. And those who repay evil for good, They oppose me, because I follow what is good. Do not forsake me, O LORD; O my God, do not be far from me! Make haste to help me, O Lord, my salvation!"

Psalm 38:1 – 22 (NASB)

_____
_____
_____
_____
_____
_____
_____
_____
_____
_____
_____
_____
_____

Set your thoughts aside for now and review them after praying and asking God what He has for you in this Psalm. After a day or so, ask your mentor and friend, the one God gave you as a partner in this journey, to discuss his or her thoughts and yours. When God brings two people together He desires that they help one another discern what He has for each of them. "Iron sharpens iron!"

What I believe defines truth for me

When a gardener spends time in the winter season evaluating the previous season, the often has questions about why the results were what they were. Was it soil conditions, infestations from insects and pests, the water quantity or the seeds that were used? During that evaluation most serious gardeners have some knowledge and experience they rely upon as being factual. Even the most experienced and skilled gardener, whose knowledge base is vast, makes some serious errors in what he believes to be true.

That is also true in many aspects of life and the challenges everyone faces in life's journey. You are the same and, perhaps, even more sure of what you believe about God, others around you, and yourself. From the very beginning of time, the enemy of our soul, Satan, has tried to convince everyone to believe lies about others, ourselves and God!

If his primary goal is to steal the glory from God and usher people into hell rather than allow them to enter heaven, lies may be the most effective weapon he has. This is especially true when we realize God gave us His Word, the Bible, through which we can know the truth and find the freedom He has for us in life.

If you continue in My word, then you are truly disciples of Mine and you will know the truth, and the truth will make you free." John 8:31b – 32 (NASB)

These are Jesus' own words to those who walked closely with Him during His earthly ministry. He was determined to teach them (and us today) that truth from God is and what prevents us from being slaves to any lie of Satan's.

"It was for freedom that Christ set us free; therefore keep standing firm and do not be subject again to a yoke of slavery." Galatians 5:1 (NASB)

Paul reminds us today that our freedom was the purpose Jesus had when He died for us to have a chance to know the truth. Being set free by Jesus was for our continued freedom by knowing truth and not by being enslaved by lies. Your addiction was, to a large part, a result of you believing lies about yourself, others and God.

You may have known Jesus before you fell into the prison of addiction, but not standing firm in those truths about life became negatively powerful. Those lies became the source of power that closed your prison doors in the past. It is time to look into your beliefs and see what God says about some of what is true in your mind.

Take a few minutes now and pray, asking God what He wants to reveal to you about what you truly believe about yourself. After praying the way you were encouraged earlier – *"Lord, I want to hear what You have for me in this time, I am ready to listen and have my paper and pencil in hand. Speak Lord!"* Write what God has shown you that you truly believe about yourself.

Are you valuable to your immediate family and close friends? Explain why you believe it is this way?

_____

_____

_____

_____

Do your friends and family truly love you? Explain why you believe it is this way?

_____

_____

_____

_____

_____

Does what you do and say have value to others? Explain why you believe it is this way?

_____

_____

_____

_____

_____

When people say things to you, do they often try to hurt you? Explain why you believe it is this way?

_____

_____

_____

_____

When you try to do good for others, does it almost always goes wrong? Explain why you believe it is this way?

_____

_____

_____

_____

God will never forgive me of what I have done in the past! Explain why you believe it is this way?

_____

_____

_____

_____

My family and friends will never trust me again! Explain why you believe it is this way?

_____

_____

_____

_____

_____

It seems as though the world is keeping me from succeeding! Explain why you believe it is this way?

_____

_____

_____

_____

_____

When you look at the history of God's people the primary weapon of the enemy is lies. Convincing the people of God that lies are "*truth*" has established the foundation for every defeat God's people have suffered, both in their personal lives and the life of the Church. Once you understand what you truly believe about yourself, you will have begun to establish the foundation of true freedom.

The war that we fight

All people on this earth today and from the beginning of time has established a set of assumptions that has guided their interpretation of their daily life. Those assumption and the experiences of daily life, the interactions with individuals and society as a whole, continue to shape and add definition to the way all of us react to events and even non-events. Those assumptions form the basis for what each one views as the realities of life. This can be simply defined as our worldview. If we have a "religion" or "faith," it helps us shape our worldview. Within that spiritual dimension of our perspective or the lack thereof, atheism, we find the filter of what we believe to be true, spiritually, humanly, and culturally. In our western worldview as Christians, we find a widely varied understanding of spiritual warfare. The range is endless, yet easily defined in three basic perspectives – 1) demonic activity ended in the time of Jesus as did the gifts of the Spirit– 2) demonic activity exists today, but the followers of Jesus have no responsibility except to love everyone and be gentle, good people – 3) war is an ongoing part of life for everyone, even the Christian, and our role is to engage actively each battle in the name of Jesus.

While there is much more to this brief description and reality, the important aspects for the journey you find yourself on today, that of finding freedom from addictions and controlling behaviors, will be what the focus is upon. After a season of freedom from what holds you in bondage, it would be of great value to spend some time exploring the deeper aspects of Spiritual warfare so that you can be further strengthened as a warrior for the Savior.

As a brief introduction to why it is important to examine your worldview and reshape it for the war you now find yourself engaged in, the beginning point is knowing God and His four most prominent names. These are names He has been given and the ones He has given Himself.

The oldest name for Him in the English language is expressed – *El* = *meaning the ultimate power of might and transcendence.* – or the greatest power ever known and beyond or above all things that are created by Him and for Him. It is a designation for deity in Babylon, Arabia, and the land of Canaan.

Next is the plural of *El* – *Elohim* = *it indicates a plural in intensity, transcendence and might.* This is the most used throughout the Bible, nearly 2,000 times in the Old Testament to refer to the God of Israel.

Third – *Adonai* = *used by the Hebrews by which God revealed Himself.* It is seldom used by any other people, just mainly by the Hebrew people.

Fourth and the final primary name – *Yahweh* – *the name unique to His covenant people.* This is the name He uses between Himself and all His covenant peoples. This is His self revealing name He proclaimed when He set and continues to set His people free from slavery.

*"Then Moses said to God, "Behold, I am going to the sons of Israel, and I will say to them, 'The God of your fathers has sent me to you.' Now they may say to me, 'What is His name?' What shall I say to them?" God said to Moses, "I AM WHO I AM"(**Yahweh**); and He said, "Thus you shall say to the sons of Israel, 'I AM (**Yahweh**) has sent me to you.'" God, furthermore, said to Moses, "Thus you shall say to the sons of Israel, 'The LORD, the God of your fathers, the God of Abraham, the God of Isaac, and the God of Jacob, has sent me to you.' This is My name forever, and this is My memorial-name to all generations" Exodus 3:13 – 15 (NASB) (**parenthesis and emphasis added are mine**)*

This has never changed nor will it change. He is the One who delivers out of slavery of all types, at all times and His name will never change. One of the last Prophets to speak before the 400 years of silence before Jesus came was Malachi. The Lord spoke through him to assure everyone that His name and His purposes never change.

"For I, the LORD, do not change" Malachi 3:6 (NASB)

Why and how are these truths so important in understanding Spiritual war? Why will the history and truth about God help me in the journey from bondage to freedom? There is more that is important to understand. Gaining that understanding of how you will become free and how you can remain free will begin to take shape, and the journey will take on a whole new dimension.

"I am the LORD your God, who brought you out of the land of Egypt, out of the house of slavery" Exodus 20:2 (NASB)

God delivered His people out of the slavery that they themselves entered into because of their disobedience. When He delivered them from that slavery at His own initiative, He began to restore the bond between Himself and His people that has been damaged in the fall. The knowledge that Adam and Eve sought in the garden, in disobedience to God's instructions, was now being restored by God through revealing His nature and character through His name.

God desires all mankind to be free from bondage and slavery, no matter what type of imprisonment or how it came about, even self-imposed slavery to substances or behaviors. **He desires to reveal Himself as the God who delivers and has given those who choose to be called His people His covenant name - *YAHWEH!***

God established personal relationship with mankind in the garden. His desire is to restore that personal relationship with those who desire to be in relationship with Him. Through the urging of the Holy Spirit and the revelation of His character and heart to those who want freedom, He provides deliverance and freedom for all who ask and do their part.

Man continues to fall into the same patterns of behavior and disobedience throughout history. Many people begin by knowing about God as the One who made heaven and earth and the One who gave him life.

Then as time moves forward and the world presses in on mankind, looking to other things as the solution to life's stresses and challenges progresses to the point where man chooses alternatives to God alone as the source of peace. The next step is that God is either completely out of the picture or the very last place man turns to get the help needed.

Substance use and abuse causes behaviors that have been introduced into our lives by others and, finally, takes the strength needed to break the yoke of slavery that is not broken, but enslaves us even more. God has warned us in His word how this downward spiral ends. His revelation as the Deliverer coupled with His warnings of what has always been the result overcomes the desires of the flesh that caused the fall. He desires to give us access to knowledge – only knowing the difference between good and evil must now originate from God and not man's choices.

"They sacrificed to demons who were not God, to gods whom they have not known, new gods who came lately, whom your fathers did not dread. You neglected the Rock who begot you, and forgot the God who gave you birth." Deuteronomy 32:17 – 17 (NASB)

The subtle nature of the evil one's tactics and the tendency of mankind to stray from the truth works together in everyone's life, when truth is not foremost in our minds daily. When the word of God is not the first thing we experience each morning and what is prominent in our lives throughout the day, we can easily start to neglect the truth as warned about in the passage above. Very few people, if any at all, make a purposeful decision to walk away from God once He has been a part of their lives. Outside influences and stress coupled with the subtle tactics the enemy uses clears a path to depending upon something that will not help or provide people with safety and security. These things who want to be god, but are not gods at all cannot deliver or provide release from bondage, especially the bondage of addictions!

As we look into the manner in which false beliefs enter our lives, keep in mind the revelation of who God revealed Himself to be – *YAHWEH – Deliverer*!

How do false beliefs begin?

As soon as Adam and Eve sinned they hid from God. The first thing He did was to ask them a question. God knew where they were, but He wanted them to realize where they were. All false beliefs are destroyed and replaced by truth when you know where you are!

Daniel L. Taylor

"They heard the sound of the LORD God walking in the garden in the cool of the day, and the man and his wife hid themselves from the presence of the LORD God among the trees of the garden. Then the LORD God called to the man, and said to him, "Where are you?" Genesis 3:8 – 9 (NASB)

By establishing what you believe about yourself you now must share that with God and another believer as the Word states. Hiding from God is not really hiding at all. That is the fundamental truth that must guide all we say and do. He knows all things and is not shocked by the lies we believe. God is not caught by surprise about anything!

When you believe a lie is the truth, you act on that foundation. Your life is then built on that foundation, which is unstable and will fall apart once stress or challenges come your way.

Knowing the enemy's tactics and strategies will equip you to fight the war and win many, if not most, of the battles that lead to life. Living with false beliefs controlling you only leads to depression and death. Even when you feel certain you know the truth, the enemy can use deceit and your own thoughts to try to trap you into thinking differently from how God views you.

Knowing the ultimate goal of the enemy is to kill, steal and destroy should cause us to be on guard. Jesus warned those He taught by identifying the true nature of the enemy.

". . . . He was a murderer from the beginning, and does not stand in the truth because there is no truth in him. Whenever he speaks a lie, he speaks from his own nature, for he is a liar and the father of lies." John 8:44 (NASB)

The very first lie the enemy uses is that your way of dealing with life's challenges and stress is the right way. Your way is better than God's way, and you are hurting no one because of the way you have chosen. The enemy can be very persuasive and convincing.

Many people follow after their own ways, and from outward appearances, their lives seem to be going well. Deep within their daily lives, things may be in terrible condition, they are just able to hide the issues better. Trying to hide the true situation was the tactic Adam and Eve did when they first disobeyed God. It led to death then and still does today!

"There is a way which seems right to a man, But its end is the way of death. Proverbs 14:12 (NASB)

If we look deeply into the original fall of mankind, we can find some of the enemy's basic tactics and methods he still uses today. Satan is not very original and isn't very smart. He is, however, cunning.

*"Then the LORD God took the man and put him into the garden of Eden to cultivate it and keep it. The LORD God commanded the man, saying, "**From any tree of the garden you may eat freely; but from the tree of the knowledge of good and evil you shall not eat**, for in the day that you eat from it you will surely die." Genesis 2:15-17 (NASB)*

Look closely and remember the instructions God gave man (*emphasis mine*). Now look deeply at the way Satan convinced them that their ways were better than God's (*emphasis mine*). As subtle as it may seem, the enemy's cunning approach to those first two of God's children remains the same today.

*"Now the serpent was more crafty than any beast of the field which the LORD God had made. And he said to the woman, "**Indeed, has God said, 'You shall not eat from any tree of the garden'**?" The <u>woman said to the serpent</u>, "From the fruit of the trees of the garden we may eat; but from the fruit of the tree which is in the middle of the garden, **God has said, 'You shall not eat from it or touch it**, or you will die.'" The serpent said to the woman, "**You surely will not die!** "For God knows that in the day you eat from it your eyes will be opened, and you will be like God, knowing good and evil."*

When the woman saw that the tree was good for food, and that it was a delight to the eyes, and that the tree was desirable to make one wise, she took from its fruit and ate; and she gave also to her husband with her, and he ate. Then the eyes of both of them were opened, and they knew that they were naked; and they sewed fig leaves together and made themselves loin coverings. Genesis 3:1 – 7 (NASB)

The first thing he will try to do is to bring doubt about what God says in His word. *"**Indeed, has God said, 'You shall not eat from any tree of the garden'**?"* When the educational system teaches the skill of persuasive speech and interaction, the principle that solidifies doubt in the mind of those who are listening is to strongly but subtly question what they think is true. Notice the strong yet subtly used in this case – *"**Indeed, has God said.**"*

Without knowing with confidence what God has said, we begin to doubt what is true and what He has said. Doubt begins to take root in our minds and our own fallen nature, inherited from those first two who fell, begins to create our own "truth" that fits what we want to be true.

The subtle nature of this doubt in this seemingly simple and harmless question is powerful when looked at closely. This is especially true if looked at from the perspective of Satan, who wants to steal all the glory from God. The implication imbedded within that question, although unsaid, is – *"God is withholding something from us, why?"* Satan's broad sweeping generalization in this case establishes the footing for the war he is assailing mankind with. Satan wishes to steal God's children away. There is a subtle difference in warfare between standing firm and holding the ground taken and conducting an assault and taking new ground. Most, if not all, warfare tactics begin with psychological warfare of some degree.

Dig to the root

What is it about God's instructions on how we should live that you began to doubt or were unsure of? What happened in your early years that established a basic foundation for the truth of God to be replaced with the lies from the enemy? In many cases, one of two things has happened that allow this to take place.

In people's lives who turns to some form of substance or behavior to cope with stress either something traumatic or wrong was imposed upon them when they were young, or something that God intended for them to have and learn was withheld. This is not a fact that will allow anyone to hide from their personal responsibility in bondage, yet it is true.

Perhaps the word of God was not an important part of your life growing up. Perhaps the word of God was involved in your life but the way it was lived out by those whom you looked up to was in contradiction to what the word said to do.

Only you can sort those two possibilities out and determine what is true in your life. But trusting in another believer and trusting the Lord with it is fundamental to the freedom you deserve and are seeking. Now look at the next tactic of the enemy once the seeds of doubt were planted and the lack of solid understanding by Eve helped those seeds to grow.

Satan did not hesitate to question the consequences of the actions he wanted them to take. *"The serpent said to the woman, "**You surely will not die!**"* While he placed even more doubt by the way he phrased the challenge, he knew that doubt had already sprouted because of the lack of true recall about what God had said. Notice the subtle strengthening of the doubt by using the persuasion tactic in the word "**surely**." The most important principle in this next step Satan uses on them and everyone today is discount or minimize the consequences of the disobedience of God's instructions. If the consequences are not pre-eminent and carefully thought out, as well as readily in mind before acting, they simply have little or no impact on our decisions.

As a simple example that perhaps may have been a part of your life in the past, think about driving while drinking. As soon as the decision to release some of the tensions or stress of life by having a few drinks came to mind, the thought of any serious consequences of that choice seldom come to mind.

The lie that a "*few drinks*" would be the limit became a truth that shut out any thoughts of arrest or accident. Once the act of drinking a few drinks began to impact the thinking process, what was irrational thinking a few hours earlier became rational thinking now. The consequences of the actions were hidden behind the lies of the enemy. "*I can handle a few more and drive home safely without incident*" is a typical rationale. Some people even begin with the thought that the "*legal limit*" was for someone else and their particular metabolism and abilities are not the same as others, they can handle alcohol better.

Now look at the response Eve gave when challenged by the enemy. God had stated His boundaries, and from all we know, man understood he was not to eat the fruit from the tree of the knowledge of good and evil. After the doubt took root in their minds, their understanding of the boundaries faded into a distortion of the truth.

"*The <u>woman said to the serpent</u>, "From the fruit of the trees of the garden we may eat; but from the fruit of the tree which is in the middle of the garden, **God has said, 'You shall not eat from it or touch it**, or you will die.*

Satan gained a tremendous foothold in this distortion of the truth because Eve's response turned from a simple distortion of truth into a lie, a false belief. With the fertile ground of doubt firmly established – "*God is withholding something from us, why?*" – the false beliefs begins to sprout and grow. In their minds the progression of this thought seemed natural – "*if God is withholding something from us, He is not Who we think He is!*".

43

For their entire time in relationship with God they never once thought He was withholding anything. They had complete access to everything they needed and could enjoy everything else within the garden. Satan knew God and knew that He had only withheld one thing from him and his legions before they rebelled – the glory due God alone. Now Satan could steal the loyalty these first two had towards God by convincing them what they needed was what God alone could provide – the knowledge of good and evil.

An Age old strategy

Satan's tactics are the same today as they were in the beginning: convince mankind that what they need is something other than dependence upon God for all they need. Addictions of all types begin with these same false beliefs. God is simply not enough to comfort and console. God is simply withholding something from me that will help me. Knowledge of God's word and dependence upon Him will not be enough. What God says is evil, man calls good. What God says is good and all sufficient, mankind says is not enough and not good enough for it.

Satan often shows us the earthly pleasures of seemingly short term disobedience without showing us the destructive nature of the long-term consequences of our choices.
The subtle practices that often have little or no consequences right away, a few drinks, a few hits of marijuana or some other drug, or dabbling with sexual pleasures outside of God's design or short term gratification through pornography will slowly lead to dependence. Once that dependence has gained prominence it becomes the place of "refuge" for the stresses of life and the place of "pleasure" and "fantasy." Soon God is no longer prominent. Without consequences for those choices, they soon become "gods which are no gods at all" and we awaken to find ourselves far from God.

*The serpent said to the woman, "**You surely will not die!** "For God knows that in the day you eat from it your eyes will be opened, and you will be like God, knowing good and evil."*

Once Satan convinces us to experiment with sin and disobedience he then uses subtle tactics already growing in our minds, doubt and our perception of love as a means to fulfill his desire, to kill us. *"**You surely will not die!**"* Notice that it was an exclamation not simply a statement. Then his next words show us that his most effective weapon in the psychology of deceitful scheming to convince us is to follow through with our disobedience.

"For God knows that in the day you eat from it your eyes will be opened, and you will be like God, knowing good and evil."

Every human since this original fall from obedience has a desire to know the mysteries of God and to be fully informed in the ways of God. The fallen human nature of every person on planet earth desires to know what God knows about the things we will encounter both now and in the future. Having our *"eyes opened"* and *"be like God, knowing good and evil"*. Especially when the opening of that statement indicates what we are doing is okay with God, even when we remember His original words, *"For God knows"*.

Everyone wants to have a special position with God. Everyone wants to think that he has a special place in God's heart. Whereas the reality of that is that everyone does have a special position with God and a special place in God's heart – it is through Jesus and obedience that we gain that place. Satan uses that truth and those desires and the false beliefs that cause us problems in life against us.

*"Has the LORD as much delight in burnt offerings and sacrifices as in obeying the voice of the LORD? **Behold, to obey is better than sacrifice**" 1 Samuel 15:22 (b) (NASB) (emphasis mine)*

The good news in knowing all these subtle tactics and understanding that everyone has false beliefs is that God knows too. He knows all things and desires that everyone should come to the knowledge of truth. He is the Deliverer and the One who gives grace to the humble who confess and repent! Not even false beliefs can block our path to freedom, but being convinced that a lie is the truth and remaining convinced will delay the grace and freedom everyone needs.

"That if you confess with your mouth Jesus as Lord, and believe in your heart that God raised Him from the dead, you will be saved" Romans 10:9 (NASB)

How do we fight and win the battle of false beliefs?

There are two primary principles about fighting the battle against false beliefs that apply to every encounter with God, the Deliverer. These two principles are the very foundational characteristics God desires in mankind, and He will honor and respond to them in all circumstances. They are also some of the hardest to integrate into our daily lives with others, as well as with God.

Because they are foundational and difficult to practice, we see God's character unfold within that contrast. Dependence upon Him and Him alone! The first principle is the Holy reverence for God as Creator of all.

"The fear of the LORD is the beginning of wisdom;" Psalm 111:10(a) (NASB)

"Fear" in this context is not being afraid of God, but having a Holy reverence and respect of His awesome power and having that tempered with awe of His willingness to give grace and mercy, to those who love Him. The second part of that is expressed in the words of David, the man after God's own heart.

"The sacrifices of God are a broken spirit; a broken and a contrite heart, O God, You will not despise." Psalm 51:17 (NASB)

The second principle for us is obedience to Him and His word.

Sacrificing things to God, giving money for His work and giving up our time to serve others is important, but not the same. What God wants more than our time, money, and resources is knowing Him deeply. He will grant us mercy, when we are more than just sorry for what we have done. God desires us to be deeply saddened by how what we have done impacts His heart and hurts Him personally. Fighting the lies of the enemy and our own false beliefs begins with pleasing Him the way He desires to be pleased.

Knowing that His heart is aching over us believing falsely about His ways and His truth begins the most effective battle tactic against the enemy who desires to *"kill, steal and destroy."* With the primary principles in place, then comes the elements with which we protect ourselves and the weapons with which we wage the war.

In Ephesians we find Paul writing to every one of us about how we can best fight the spiritual war we face daily. Knowing the basics about the armor of God is important. Armor is one of the basic elements that protects the warriors who fight wars of every type. Knowing what that armor consists of as well as how to put it on is critical for the ultimate protection it brings in every type of war. In spiritual warfare it is especially important because much of the war consists of "unseen" forces.

Even before the soldier puts on the battle armor, he must first get conditioned and ready to fight by conditioning his body and mind. That is why God has shown us what He says is the beginning of wisdom: the fear of the Lord. Paul spoke into the lives of God's people at Ephesus some very important principles about winning the war of truth before he began to instruct them about the protections God offers His own.

*"Therefore **I ask you not to lose heart at my tribulations on your behalf, for they are your glory. For this reason I bow my knees before the Father**, from whom every family in heaven and on earth derives its name, **that He would grant you,** according to the riches of His glory, **to be strengthened with power through His Spirit in the inner man**, so that Christ may dwell in your hearts through faith; and **that you, being rooted and grounded in love, may be able to comprehend with all the saints** what is the breadth and length and height and depth, and to know the love of Christ which surpasses knowledge, **that you may be filled up to all the fullness of God**. Now to Him who is able to do far more abundantly beyond all that we ask or think, according to the power that works within us, to Him be the glory in the church and in Christ Jesus to all generations forever and ever. Amen" Ephesians 3:13 – 21 (NASB)(emphasis mine)*

Notice how Paul tells us not to be discouraged when the war rages around us and the attacks come in our direction. He lets us see the first step in conditioning our hearts and minds according to the principles God desires in us – humility before God. The picture that comes to mind for many when the term "humility" is used is embarrassment or someone being weak. In God's economy, weakness in the human realm means God's strength and power can be better manifested through His desire for us to allow Him to be our **Deliverer**.

The strengthening of the inner man to trust Him and not our own strength is the result of true humility before the One Who has the power we need. That power is far beyond all we could ever have from any other source. Remember the first name of God *"El"* – meaning more powerful than any other power and above and beyond all that He created!

Our human, fallen spirit is in a constant battle against the indwelling Holy Spirit to define truth. Our own nature wants to decide the difference between good and evil and choose which is which independent of anyone else. Even God! So when our inner man is strengthened through His Spirit's work within us, our trust in Him grows. In that strengthening process we find our own desires grow to be firmly rooted and grounded by growing in the desire to please God more than self. The truth about who God is and the reality of being aware of how much He desires to defend and protect us when the evil one battle against us brings freedom beyond our imagination.

When we finally begin to comprehend that the power we need comes from God and not our own strength or as defined by our own truths, which are usually not truth but lies, we join the ranks of history with other saints. Once that comprehension takes root, we are more likely to allow ourselves to trust God in a more complete and full way daily.

Now that the Lord has done His work in our minds and conditioned us to trust Him by humbling ourselves and being broken enough to admit our ways are leading to destruction, He is ready to show us more of His ways. Notice the closing of Paul's instruction to the believers in Ephesus. It is all for the glory of God and not for man to brag about or to take credit for, which catches the evil one off guard. Once we begin to learn how to condition our hearts and minds and then give God all the glory for what has been accomplished, Satan knows he is losing the battle.

That means we need to rely upon more of God's protection and power because the war will increase in intensity, which equates to our understanding that our true strength comes from God.

With the conditioning underway, God also provides everyone who desires to access it, protective "armor" through His word and teaches us how to practice God's principles and ways. One of the ways Paul tells the Ephesians and all of us today is by our being with other believers as often as possible.

"Therefore I, the prisoner of the Lord, implore you to walk in a manner worthy of the calling with which you have been called, with all humility and gentleness, with patience, showing tolerance for one another in love, being diligent to preserve the unity of the Spirit in the bond of peace. There is one body and one Spirit, just as also you were called in one hope of your calling; one Lord, one faith, one baptism, one God and Father of all who is over all and through all and in all." Ephesians 4:1-6 (NASB)

The plea is not just a simple suggestion but a very strong instruction to *"walk in a manner worthy of the calling with which you have been called."* What follows that instruction is how we can best do that "walking" or living that out in our lives each day. It may seem impossible at first, but it is not only possible, it becomes easier the more we practice it.

*"With **all humility and gentleness, with patience, showing tolerance for one another in love, being diligent to preserve the unity of the Spirit in the bond of peace.** There is one body and one Spirit, just as also you were called in one hope of your calling; one Lord,*

one faith, one baptism, one God and Father of all who is over all and through all and in all." "(Ephesians 4:2-6 (NASB)) Being humble and gentle, patiently tolerant of everyone we encounter, is the first step in building on the power Jesus provides. It is also what true love mandates, when we look at how Jesus loved all He encountered. If our goal is to grow in being like Jesus, then our behavior and attitude must be modeled after Him.

God strengthens everyone who desires to model Jesus' behaviors and attitudes and empowers them to grow even more. "***Being diligent to preserve the unity of the Spirit in the bond of peace"*** indicates an intentional act of our will is required even when we think otherwise.

Denying "self" and preserving unity or oneness is a true outward act of the inner attitude of humility that the Lord is developing within those who desire it. That is only possible through the work of the indwelling Holy Spirit, which brings the "peace" spoken of by Paul in this instruction to us. The "bond of peace" grows as we deny our own selfish nature and we love others the way Jesus loved us and everyone on earth. He denied Himself so greatly that He died for us to provide eternity with Him!

Paul then finishes this portion of our conditioning exercise and preparation for fighting the war by reminding us all about why unity is important in our lives and the lives of all who believe. *"There is one body and one Spirit, just as also you were called in one hope of your calling; one Lord, one faith, one baptism, one God and Father of all who is over all and through all and in all."* God the Father, God the Son and God the Holy Spirit are one in heart, mind and purpose and they establish the examples we need to follow. Whereas it may be difficult to understand, it is very important simply to trust in that truth as believers!

The importance of being involved in a Church and fellowshipping with other believers cannot be overstated. In that conditioning for the spiritual war we are engaged in, being with other believers helps us learn how to give and receive grace. It helps us to practice loving others, even when they are not easy to love. It also sharpens our eyes, ears, and hearts to hear the voice of God through our brothers and sisters while we learn how to strengthen ourselves and others through prayer.

"Finally, be strong in the Lord and in the strength of His might. Put on the full armor of God, so that you will be able to stand firm against the schemes of the devil. For our struggle is not against flesh and blood, but against the rulers, against the powers, against the world forces of this darkness, against the spiritual forces of wickedness in the heavenly places.

Therefore, take up the full armor of God, so that you will be able to resist in the evil day, and having done everything, to stand firm. Stand firm therefore, HAVING GIRDED YOUR LOINS WITH TRUTH, and HAVING PUT ON THE BREASTPLATE OF RIGHTEOUSNESS, and having shod YOUR FEET WITH THE PREPARATION OF THE GOSPEL OF PEACE; in addition to all, taking up the shield of faith with which you will be able to extinguish all the flaming arrows of the evil one. And take THE HELMET OF SALVATION, and the sword of the Spirit, which is the word of God. Ephesians 6:10 – 17 (NASB)

The very first and perhaps most important instruction Paul gives us involves where our strength comes from. Many ask God to "strengthen" them. The idea sounds great and in many aspects the request is good, but being strong in and of ourselves can be a problem. Soon, we would not think we need the Lord as much and then the subtle drift plus the lies of the enemy can cause us to fall into problems. The proper prayer is to ask the Lord to be our strength.

Notice how Paul phrases this instruction – *"Finally, be strong in the Lord and in the strength of His might"*. Our strength should be to keep our focus upon God and His word. Being "strong in the Lord" implies we turn to Him in all ways and at all times. Notice also that we are to add to our singular focus *"the strength of His might."* His might is stronger than anything man can muster up on his own.

What will protect us when the fight gets tougher than expected?

The enemy has no sense of appropriateness in his battle tactics. Like earthly terrorists, Satan and his demons do all they can to cause God's children to live in fear. Being able to disrupt the daily life of followers of the Lord and causing them to be fearful is the easiest way to take back the ground Satan has lost. God now gives Paul the insights about being victorious when the battle gets tougher than we expected.

"Put on the full armor of God, so that you will be able to stand firm against the schemes of the devil. For our struggle is not against flesh and blood, but against the rulers, against the powers, against the world forces of this darkness, against the spiritual forces of wickedness in the heavenly places. Therefore, take up the full armor of God, so that you will be able to resist in the evil day, and having done everything, to stand firm. Stand firm therefore, HAVING GIRDED YOUR LOINS WITH TRUTH, and HAVING PUT ON THE BREASTPLATE OF RIGHTEOUSNESS, and having shod YOUR FEET WITH THE PREPARATION OF THE GOSPEL OF PEACE; in addition to all, taking up

the shield of faith with which you will be able to extinguish all the flaming arrows of the evil one. And take THE HELMET OF SALVATION, *and the sword of the Spirit, which is the word of God." Ephesians 6:11 – 17 (NASB)*

The very first thing that everyone who has been set free should be aware of is Who supplies the protections against the enemy. Like the Lord's strength, His armor is what is needed, not our own defenses or means of protection – *"Put on the full armor **of God**."*

God created all things and His power is without weakness. When He supplies His followers with protections, such as this *"full armor,"* it is more than just figurative in nature, it is real! Its purpose is to give us the ability to remain free from the bondages that have been imprisoning us for too long. Jesus sets us free so that we can remain free and join the battle to set others free.

The armor He provides is one source of protection – *"against the rulers, against the powers, against the world forces of this darkness, against the spiritual forces of wickedness in the heavenly places."* Our tendency is to fight our battles against what we can see, hear, touch, and interact with. That is only part of who the spiritual battle is against. The real battle is waged *"in the heavenly places."* But we, as earthly bound fleshly beings who are truly spiritual beings that simply inhabit the flesh while on this earth, must come to the understanding of our limitations. Even those closest to Jesus had the same struggle.

"It is the Spirit who gives life; the flesh profits nothing; the words that I have spoken to you are spirit and are life. But there are some of you who do not believe." John 6:63 & 64 (NASB)

One of the most underused and least thought about part of the "full armor of God" is the gift of grace. Jesus came to give us many gifts, but the first gift that should be used in the war when it gets tougher than we expect is the grace of repentance. If you think the gift of repentance is not a gift of grace, "the gift that is undeserved and unable to be earned," then think again. God is just – meaning all that deserves punishment will receive punishment. He is also Holy. If those two truths are foundational, and they are, then the gift of repentance – turning away from sin and disobedience and being fully restored – because we ask for it, is granted because of what Jesus did for us. That is definitely grace! Repentance is often uncomfortable and difficult to accomplish for most; it establishes the ground to fight the war upon. In military tactics, the winner is the side that chooses where the fight takes place. The same is true in spiritual war.

Daniel L. Taylor

By first approaching the Lord, asking Him what is displeasing to Him and then confessing our own sins, the ground on which we can fight the battle becomes Holy ground. It establishes the characteristics of the battle tactics as well as the battleground. With the principles of God guiding our every action, we find His strength replacing our own perceived strength.

Being aligned with God's principles and being "clean before the father" through confession will put the enemy in his place, defeated and unable to bring accusations that are valid.

"I have listened to the voice of the LORD my God; ***I have done according to all that You have commanded me****. 'Look down from Your holy habitation, from heaven, and bless Your people Israel, and the ground which You have given us . ." Deuteronomy 26:15 a (NASB)*

The second most important part of *"the full armor of God"* are the prayers of the brothers and sisters. Unity in all things is a wonderful and underrated gift from God. The strength of each individual prayer has great value and power. God provides His power when we pray to Him with clean hands and a clean heart. When we ask our brothers and sisters to pray on our behalf two things are accomplished – the outcome will be according to the will of God and, secondly, we further acknowledge to God and the brothers and sisters that we are weak, so His strength can be made perfect.

"Therefore I am well content with weaknesses, with insults, with distresses, with persecutions, with difficulties, ***for Christ's sake; for when I am weak, then I am strong****." 2 Corinthians 12:10 (NASB)*

*"****Is anyone among you suffering****? Then he must pray. Is anyone cheerful? He is to sing praises. Is anyone among you sick? Then he must call for the elders of the church and they are to pray over him, anointing him with oil in the name of the Lord; and the prayer offered in faith will restore the one who is sick, and the Lord will raise him up, and if he has committed sins, they will be forgiven him. Therefore,* ***confess your sins to one another, and pray for one another so that you may be healed. The effective prayer of a righteous man can accomplish much****." James 5:13 – 16 (NASB)*

Be aware that prayers spoken in less than full, complete belief will not be as effective. The battle tactics of the enemy are very similar to terrorists. Terrorists are trying to instill in those who he wishes to control fear, doubt and unbelief. When we are instructed *"having done everything, to stand firm"* we must stand in faith that God is already aware we are under attack.

Once these first two critical steps are taken, then the battle moves from taking new ground toward holding the ground already taken by God. When Paul used the image of putting on God's armor he was intentional about his beginning *"HAVING GIRDED YOUR LOINS WITH TRUTH."*

When someone "girds their loins" in today's language, he is putting on a belt. A belt holds everything else worn together and in proper alignment. The phrase literally means in order to put on the "armor" of God, the most important element that holds that armor all together and provides protection is "**truth**". When anyone wearing armor "girds his loins," he is putting on what holds the armor in place so he is fully protected by God's truth no matter how tough the battle gets.

If you think back at how the behaviors and substances you used formerly and now struggle with began, as well as how those coping mechanisms got totally out of control, it was through false beliefs. Only the "truth can set us free," as the word states – the truth about who we are and what purposes God has for us. It is the truth about who God is in reality and not some distorted fantasy. It's the truth about how the world operates around us and impacts our lives, often driving us away from living the way He designed us. Standing firm and letting all those truths and many more, hold "the armor of God" together will set us free.

So when we look at that foundation of truth, next we can better understand how God chooses to provide us with protection for our "hearts." He next tells us *"HAVING PUT ON THE BREASTPLATE OF RIGHTEOUSNESS."* When thinking about righteousness, most begin with our own definition of what righteous is. Understanding that we are fighting a war against the enemy, we should begin to set aside our own understandings, such as our definition of righteousness, and look into His word as our source. What does God say about righteousness?

The first mention of the word "righteousness" comes in Genesis 15. Abram and his wife were old and unable to have children. There was a war going on among nine different kings. One group defeated the other group because they had the advantage. As a result of this war, Abram's nephew Lot and his people were taken captive. Abram wanted to find them and set them free. He gathered together his people and defeated those who held Lot, Abrams nephew and set them all free. He also gathered a great deal of plunder in the process.

When the king of Sodom came out to thank Abram, he brought with him the king of Salem (what became and is now Jerusalem, chosen city of God). Satan wanted to disrupt Abram's righteous lifestyle, so he used the king of Sodom's offer of wealth to tempt him. Abram refused the offer and "stood firm" in the truth of God, which meant the people were more important than the possessions and wealth. Does that sound familiar?

During this time of testing, Abram believed God and His promises of children and wealth beyond what he could imagine, even though he and his wife were at an old age. He had just turned down an offer of earthly wealth. God "reckoned it to him as righteousness."

*After these things the word of the LORD came to Abram in a vision, saying, "Do not fear, Abram, I am a shield to you; Your reward shall be very great." Abram said, "O Lord GOD, what will You give me, since I am childless, and the heir of my house is Eliezer of Damascus?" And Abram said, "Since You have given no offspring to me, one born in my house is my heir." Then behold, the word of the LORD came to him, saying, "This man will not be your heir; but one who will come forth from your own body, he shall be your heir." And He took him outside and said, "Now look toward the heavens, and count the stars, if you are able to count them." And He said to him, "So shall your descendants be." **Then he believed in the LORD; and He reckoned it to him as righteousness.**" Genesis 15:1 – 6 (NASB)*

Believing God's truths and promises are the beginning of righteousness, as God defines it. While none of us can be fully righteous, especially in our own efforts, believing God is the foundation of His righteousness. If we believe God at all times and in all things, then our heart will be protected because we will have put on *"breastplate of righteousness."*

That breastplate covers the heart with the righteousness of God and is always critical to have on, yet when the heart is weakened by the fierce attack, the protection is even more critical!

"Stand firm therefore ... and having shod YOUR FEET WITH THE PREPARATION OF THE GOSPEL OF PEACE"...

When warriors went into battle, their focus was primarily upon the enemy warriors and their weapons. Oftentimes in war the enemy will set traps that will injure the legs and feet of the other side and, thus, disable their mobility. When in battle every warrior must remain as mobile and agile as possible. How does this apply to the fight against the enemy we fight in this battle? When Paul wrote to the Churches at Ephesus and admonished them to have their *"feet shod with the gospel of peace"* he was encouraging them to protect themselves from being immobilized by hidden weapons. Warriors of Paul's day wore greaves and hardened shoe covers. Greaves and show covers were made of metal or thick leather so when they encountered the weapons of mobility, the warriors would not be disabled.

How do we have *"feet shod with the gospel of peace"* in our battle? What are those protective "greaves" in our day and age? How can the *"gospel of peace"* protect our mobility? When Jesus instituted the Church, He not only encouraged righteousness in every follower, He also required us to be united in all we do and say.

"For everyone will be salted with fire. "Salt is good; but if the salt becomes unsalty, with what will you make it salty again? Have salt in yourselves, and be at peace with one another." Matthew 9:49 – 50 (NASB)

Salt enhances the "flavor" and makes the food taste more desirable. By thinking about the implications of Jesus' admonition to "have salt in yourselves" what He was saying meant for us to live and relate in such a way that the peace and grace we give one another enhances all of our lives. Having our *"feet shod with the gospel of peace"* brings other believers into the battle when the enemy tries to disable our mobility.

Moving away from addictions or behaviors that are wrong in God's eyes means we must be moving toward something. God desires us to be moving toward thinking and doing what is right in His eyes.

Jesus knew how living together in peace and supporting one another during the battles we face in life would require peace among His followers. When we have *"feet shod with the gospel of peace"* we are able to protect one another from Satan's hidden weapon – division and conflict. Conflicts will arise, but giving one another grace and always allowing love to prevail will allow those conflicts to be resolved quicker and completely.

Paul stated to the Church in Corinth in its time of divisions and troubles how living at peace with one another fights the battle against satan and his ways.

"But one whom you forgive anything, I forgive also; for indeed what I have forgiven, if I have forgiven anything, I did it for your sakes in the presence of Christ, so that no advantage would be taken of us by Satan, for we are not ignorant of his schemes." 2 Corinthians 2:10-11 (NASB)

Paul brings closure to the "full armor of God" by teaching how our faith in God and not other things can take the "sting" out of satan's attack. That faith is the shield that not only takes the sting out of the attacks we encounter, but also takes the "fire" out of the experiences we have used instead of turning to God.

Those "fires" are the driving force of our relapses into the old ways. We remember those times to be exciting, numbing, and pleasurable, when in fact they were not. Satan will help us believe the lies by taking away all the troubling things that resulted in coping with stress the old way, by blanking out the bad and amplifying the supposed pleasures. When Paul summed up the full armor in this way, he understood the fallen nature of man's ways and the pleasures of the flesh, when, in fact, those things were not pleasurable at all, when they originate from sinful choices.

"In addition to all, taking up the shield of faith with which you will be able to extinguish all the flaming arrows of the evil one." Ephesians 6:16 (NASB)

Finally God, through Paul, reminds us of how He has designed us to change the way we think. When we begin to be "transformed by the renewing of our mind" in our learning new ways of thinking, we turn to God instead of our old ways of coping.

And take THE HELMET OF SALVATION, *and the sword of the Spirit, which is the word of God."Ephesians 6:17 (NASB)*

Remembering that we have been "saved" by making the commitment to Jesus as Lord and Savior, we turn to the word of God instead of our own thinking and past when we face difficulties and in everyday life. Before starting to read the word of God, praying and asking the Holy Spirit to show us what He has for us opens our hearts and minds to His revelation. Not every revelation from God, through the Holy Spirit comes with a dramatic, "spiritual" aura or experience. Oftentimes the word God wants to emphasize or the principle He wants to teach us simply stands out as important in our reading.

By beginning our time in His word by asking the Holy Spirit to reveal His truth to us while we read, we oftentimes gain much more than simply through a study originating from our own desires or as an assigned time of study. A word of caution is important here. God will never force us to learn or believe His truth. He wants our hearts and minds to desire it. He will also never deliver us from something we do not truly desire to be delivered from. He is all powerful, but He controls His use of that power in our time of transformation by His love. No one can be forced to love another, so it is with God.

Seasons of *Change*

How to prepare for new growth

Seeds of things to come

Now that the fruit of the past choices has been evaluated and the causes have been established, how can the results bring better fruit? As with every season God has given us, either in the garden, our personal lives, or our relationships, He wants new growth for us. New growth in the area of our past poor choices means new ways of approaching everything about our lives. In the end stages of winter, the gardener begins to look at the seed catalogues and he plans how the garden should be arranged. Gardeners nearly always learn from their past mistakes in where things were planted, what variety was used in the previous season, and the condition of the soil. Jesus teaches in a parable about sowing and soils and how to get fantastic new growth from the efforts.

"behold, the sower went out to sow; and as he sowed, some seeds fell beside the road, and the birds came and ate them up. Others fell on the rocky places, where they did not have much soil; and immediately they sprang up, because they had no depth of soil. But when the sun had risen, they were scorched; and because they had no root, they withered away. Others fell among the thorns, and the thorns came up and choked them out. And others fell on the good soil and yielded a crop, some a hundredfold, some sixty, and some thirty. He who has ears, let him hear." Matthew 13:3b – 9 (NASB)

He finishes with a very strong statement that everyone who knows Jesus should take to heart every day. *"He who has ears, let him hear."* What Jesus is saying is easily simplified in today's understanding – "If you truly want to learn how to live well, listen and be sure while you are listening, hear what He says." There is a difference between listening to something and hearing what is said and meant.

The listening is a function of the mechanical structures of the ears – sounds vibrate the mechanical devices within the ear and nerves send it to the proper place in the brain. Hearing what you are listening to means thinking about it, learning the lessons being taught and remembering to apply it in real life.

Jesus' parable applies to the new plans and new ways of learning now that the past is better understood. Notice Jesus brings our attention to the type of soils that have been "sown into" by the one sowing the seeds. The lesson to learn that will help continue in the new found freedom is simple. The "soil" is what provides nutrition and solid foundation from which to grow – continuing in the study of God's word and surrounded by believers in the Church in which God has planted you is extremely important for continued success. There are many more lessons that are essential in this passage which will be detailed and explained later.

Many gardeners keep journals and records of their garden's activities and outcomes. Even when they have a terrible season and the fruit was poor quality and a small harvest, they record it. Then as they plan their new garden and new season, they review it before planning for the next season.

Like the gardener, it is time to review the fruits of the past and the lessons learned. Stop now, set aside your thoughts for this new season of growth for a moment and re-read your responses up to this point. Pray and ask God what He wants to show you about your responses and, like suggested before, get you pencil and paper ready and tell Him –

"Holy Spirit, I want you to teach me what you want me to know. You promised You would reveal truth to me if I asked. I am asking You now! Father God, You promised if I asked for wisdom that you would provide me with wisdom from your storehouse of wisdom, I am asking for wisdom right now! Lord Jesus, You said You would always be there for me, I am asking that You be there for me right now!"

Now review and note what the Holy Spirit says to you and "***have ears to hear***" as Jesus taught us. After spending about 30 to 45 minutes reviewing everything you have written up to this point, set it aside, take a walk in the fresh air, and pray for clarity of understanding. When you sit back down, write on the following page what you have heard, and what you think about what you read and heard from God. Once you are finished, share it with the mentor and trusted friend God has provided for you. Share your heart openly and honestly and spend as much time as necessary to learn and grow from your experiences – mistakes and all.

"For the word of God is living and active and sharper than any two-edged sword, and piercing as far as the division of soul and spirit, of both joints and marrow, and able to judge the thoughts and intentions of the heart. [13]And there is no creature hidden from His sight, but all things are open and laid bare to the eyes of Him with whom we have to do."
Hebrews 4:12 – 13 (NASB)

Planning and anticipating new growth

The hope of better fruit

Remember, God's word is truth and His counsel is sure. He is the author and designer of mankind as well as the Creator. He has established a time for everything, and we can either live in that understanding or face certain troubles through our disobedience and independence.

"There is an appointed time for everything. And there is a time for every event under heaven - A time to give birth and a time to die; A time to plant and a time to uproot what is planted. A time to kill and a time to heal; A time to tear down and a time to build up. A time to weep and a time to laugh; A time to mourn and a time to dance. A time to throw stones and a time to gather stones; A time to embrace and a time to shun embracing. A time to search and a time to give up as lost; A time to keep and a time to throw away. A time to tear apart and a time to sew together;

A time to be silent and a time to speak. A time to love and a time to hate; A time for war and a time for peace." Ecclesiastes 3:1-8 (NASB)

When someone continues to do the same things over and over again and expects to have a different outcome, many people call it "crazy." God states His perspective and calls it being a fool, then adds another dimension of understanding of those who repeated their actions by warning us that if we think we are wise in how we approach the issue of change, then the fool has more hope.

"Like a dog that returns to its vomit, is a fool who repeats his folly. Do you see a man wise in his own eyes? There is more hope for a fool than for him. *Proverbs26:11-12 (NASB)*

For centuries, mankind has been given the instruction for how to change the results of disobedience and idolatry, but driven by false beliefs and foolish choices, many choose to do it their way instead of God's way. Once the "old fruit" has been experienced and the desire to be transformed by thinking differently (Romans 12:2) has become important in life, new plans need to be the first step in the new freedom.

With a mentor and friend who knows the details of the past and wants the very best, you have an advantage. Ask him or her to be available to guide you, counsel you and pray with you regularly. God would always encourage you to look together to Him and His word often. Once that has begun, write down what the word God brought to mind, share it with your mentor and pray together about the new plan. Jesus made us a promise about this method of Him bringing good to us all, when we follow His words and ways.

"So I say to you, ask, and it will be given to you; seek, and you will find; knock, and it will be opened to you. For everyone who asks, receives; and he who seeks, finds; and to him who knocks, it will be opened". Luke 11:9-10 (NASB)

Jesus simply reminded us that the love of God and the gifts of God bring change, when we truly seek to live according to His design and His ways. New ways of thinking and new ways of acting in every circumstance are the goals in our Christian life. Now that the season of new thinking and new planning has come about, the enemy wishes to stop us and lure us back into the old ways. He will try to steal our faith and our trust in God through many ways: doubt, fear, unbelief, temptation, and circumstances where stress begins to take control of our decisions.

How much faith do you now have in His desire to change you? An equally important question to ask yourself: how much faith do you have in your own desire to partner with God and change yourself? The element of doubt frequently begins in many of us as a question: "How much power is He willing to share with me when I need it?" Honestly begin to set the stage for a better mentoring relationship by sharing your thoughts on these questions and thoughts with your mentor.

Daniel L. Taylor

The journey to full freedom can often be similar to the journey from unhealthy living to healthy living. Once an honest look at the reality of our physical conditions is made and we are able to admit to ourselves and others how "out of shape" we truly are, the most important step in the journey is made. Then the new way of living can be shaped and looked at daily. The next step in changing your physical health is to go to the gym and test your current condition. It is the same with the journey from bondage to some form of addiction toward total freedom through the Lord. Spend some time in the "spiritual, soul gym" by honestly answering the following questions and writing it down.

"Ask, and it will be given to you; seek, and you will find; knock, and it will be opened to you. For everyone who asks receives, and he who seeks finds, and to him who knocks it will be opened" Matthew 7:7-8 (NASB)

Do you have any doubts about being able to continue to live free from the bondages of your past addictions or behaviors? If so, try to measure the amount of doubt against the amount of confidence in being successful in living free of them!

_____

_____

_____

_____

_____

_____

_____

_____

_____

_____

Doubt is a constant enemy of our faith and our ability to change. Did you consider the fact that you have begun two critical relationships – 1) With Jesus Christ – 2) with a mentor and Church that truly loves you and will walk beside you? If you can honestly say none or very little, you are far better off than many believers.

"Therefore, since we have a great high priest who has passed through the heavens, Jesus the Son of God, let us hold fast our confession. For we do not have a high priest who cannot sympathize with our weaknesses, but One who has been tempted in all things as we are, yet

without sin. Therefore let us draw near with confidence to the throne of grace, so that we may receive mercy and find grace to help in time of need." Hebrews 4:14-16 (NASB)

How many times do thoughts of your past failures come to mind in a day or week? How often do those thoughts cause you to begin to think about how hard this journey will be? Do those thoughts lead to fear or cause anxiety?

_____

_____

_____

_____

_____

_____

_____

_____

_____

_____

Past failures or less than successful outcomes bring about emotions that are often pushed out of our conscience understanding. Past events have often been pushed down for so long that they own or at least control our patterns of thinking. Denial of the true emotion becomes a natural way of life for us. This can be destructive and sabotage our new thinking patterns or it can become a great tool for success. Each individual has the choice and freedom to decide which it will be. Choose that it becomes a tool for success.

The past was not totally a failure, no matter what you think about the current situation! The old pattern of thinking and the doubts can be coupled with truth and be used against the enemy and your own emotions. Take some time and list two bad decisions from your past in simple terms. Now pray and ask God what a better decision or perhaps the best decision could have been, had you thought it through at that time.

I made a bad decision when I . .

_____

_____

_____

_____

_____

Pray a simple prayer with your whole heart and expect God to speak to you about the options you would have had back then. Remember, remind the Holy Spirit that you have your pen and paper ready and you truly want to hear His answer, and you are ready to write it down! The best decision I could have made, or at least a better decision would have been . .

_____

_____

_____

_____

_____

_____

_____

_____

_____

_____

Once we are aware of our past and have thought through those decisions and discovered what a better or the best decisions could have been, we are ready to start changing the "soil" of our planting. We can know for certain what the fruit of the future will be, if we stay on guard against going back into the hands of the enemy, even when the enemy was often our own thinking.

"As for me, I shall call upon God, and the LORD will save me at evening and morning and at noon, I will complain and murmur, and He will hear my voice. He will redeem my soul in peace from the battle which is against me" Psalm 55:16-18b (NASB)

Why is this important? Any gardener who has examined the fruit of the past and wishes to improve the nutrition and quality of the next season's planting will first prepare the soil. The soil of your heart will need the same consideration. By examining what your emotions are masking, you are trying to discover what types of improvements will bring lasting improvement. In that same analogy of the gardener and his soil being improved, it is easy to buy synthetic fertilizer and improve the soil for a season of growth, but what is far better is to use what is natural so the improvement will last for the lifetime of the garden. Like emotions masking your true heart, using synthetic fertilizers or soil conditioning agents simply cover over the real problem. No one wants to live life that way. If alcohol was the controlling factor, simply stopping drinking does not change anything other than you no longer drink; you likely still will act the same as always. The world terms that as being a "dry drunk!" That will eventually yield the same outcomes as before and will most likely lead to going back into the bondage of the past, only worse.

"Any kingdom divided against itself is laid waste; and a house divided against itself falls."
Matthew 11:17b (NASB)

If one part of us wants to be free from the bondage of addictions and another part, even below our level of conscious thoughts, wants a different outcome, failure is certain. Becoming mature in our Christian life is a life-long process, but growing beyond having a divided spirit in many areas comes much easier than many think possible. The end of Jesus' statement that began in Matthew 11:17b sheds some light on how much worse it can get. Yet even though this truth has been proven over and over again, the hope and power the Holy Spirit provides will prevail, should we choose.

"When the unclean spirit goes out of a man, it passes through waterless places seeking rest, and not finding any, it says, 'I will return to my house from which I came.' "And when it comes, it finds it swept and put in order. Then it goes and takes along seven other spirits more evil than itself, and they go in and live there; and the last state of that man becomes worse than the first" Matthew 11:24-26 (NASB)

Before getting discouraged by the truth that it will get seven times worse, there is an alternative. Filling up that emptiness with God and His word will provide the power to resist this enemy and, at the same time, will enable total victory in many other aspects of life and the choices that are made.

"For if you are careful to keep all this commandment which I am commanding you to do, to love the LORD your God, to walk in all His ways and hold fast to Him, then the LORD will drive out all these nations from before you, and you will dispossess nations greater and mightier than you. Every place on which the sole of your foot treads shall be yours" Deuteronomy 11:22-24b (NASB)

Jesus made the truth known to us toward the end of His earthly ministry, and it is a truth that overwhelms many who have walked diligently with Him for many years. It is very important to hold fast to the truth above and the truth Jesus speaks about in what we are capable of, should we choose to believe Him!

"Do you not believe that I am in the Father, and the Father is in Me? The words that I say to you I do not speak on My own initiative, but the Father abiding in Me does His works. Believe Me that I am in the Father and the Father is in Me; otherwise believe because of the works themselves. Truly, truly, I say to you, he who believes in Me, the works that I do, he will do also; and greater works than these he will do; because I go to the Father. Whatever you ask in My name, that will I do, so that the Father may be glorified in the Son. If you ask Me anything in My name, I will do it. If you love Me, you will keep My commandments." John 14:10-15 (NASB)

Another important aspect of this season of "preparing the soil" for new growth and better fruit is removing the "stones and hardened ground" left behind by the past. What are those "stones and hardened ground" made of? Broken relationships and a lack of prayer. These are two fundamentally important aspects for new growth, once the fears and doubts are identified. Prayer and attempting to reconcile past damaged relationships go hand in hand and are the "natural fertilizing agents." God intended them to be an important part of our lives in order to promote healthy growth. Oftentimes those fears and doubts are directly connected with past damaged relationships, even though if may not be seen easily.

Keeping in mind that the profession of faith in Jesus is the most important preparation and should always be in our minds, others may not have forgiven the past as readily and freely as Jesus did. Now that you have set aside a time of regularly meeting with your mentor and perhaps been involved more with your new Church family, your foundational relationships are in place for the next step.

"Rejoice always; pray without ceasing; in everything give thanks; for this is God's will for you in Christ Jesus. Do not quench the Spirit" 1 Thessalonians 5:16-19 (NASB)

Spend some time praying with your mentor and others whom you have grown to trust and love, asking God to show you through the Holy Spirit who you may have offended or damaged your relationships with. Spend some time talking over the list over with your mentor and other trusted advisors within the Church you have chosen. Write the names on a list and the offense you perceive happened or the way the relationships were damaged. Keep that list private and share it only with the Lord and your mentor.

_____

_____

_____

_____

_____

_____

_____

_____

_____

_____

Now take that list and ask the Lord who He would have you approach first to seek forgiveness and attempt reconciliation with, but do not act until you are certain and your mentor is certain you are ready. Knowing the "who" is much different from knowing the "how" and "when." Many mature Christians have attempted to reconcile damaged relationships at the wrong time and in the wrong manner. God is clear that it is important and must be done, but He is also very clear that it must be done with the right frame of mind and at the right time.

"Pursue peace with all men, and the sanctification without which no one will see the Lord. [15]See to it that no one comes short of the grace of God; that no root of bitterness springing up causes trouble, and by it many be defiled;" Hebrews 12:14-15 (NASB)

Prayer is foundational and should become the core of all we do as believers. Many who have been believers for some time still do all they can themselves first and then seek the Lord in prayer afterward. For many that has become a habit and needs to be worked on and changed. Prayer should be the primary thing all believers turn to first and foremost and must become the "new habit" or new pattern of life.

Many have said that in order to develop a new habit and forsake an old habit, the new must be practiced for 21 days in a row. It would be best if it were practiced for more than that, but that is a good starting point. Now is the perfect time, during this time of preparing your "soil" for new growth and better fruit to begin that very important practice.

Take the list of damaged relationships and what you perceive to be the cause of the offense and bring it before the Lord for the next 30 days, at least once per day. In that time be sure and let the Holy Spirit know at the very beginning of each time in prayer that you do not know what to do. Let Him know that you understand He does, and you have your pencil and paper ready to write down what He says to you.

Spend some time every day, if possible, speaking with and praying with your mentor also. The Holy Spirit will speak to him and others whom you know and trust in this new phase of your life. It has been promised and can be trusted without doubt.

"Again I say to you, that if two of you agree on earth about anything that they may ask, it shall be done for them by My Father who is in heaven. For where two or three have gathered together in My name, I am there in their midst." Matthew 18:19-20 (NASB)

Not only will the Lord help you better understand His will during a time in prayer for this issue, but also for all other matters. Developing a prayer life is a very important aspect of becoming free and staying free from the bondages of all forms of addictions and abhorrent behaviors. Prayer is one of the most important "soil conditioners" and the primary means of removing "rocks and hardened ground" in your new season and beyond. Fallow ground is ground that has been unused and trampled down through misuse and needs to be broken up and softened.

"Sow with a view to righteousness, Reap in accordance with kindness; Break up your fallow ground, For it is time to seek the LORD Until He comes to rain righteousness on you. You have plowed wickedness, you have reaped injustice, You have eaten the fruit of lies." Hosea 10:12-13a (NASB)

One word of caution as you look to others for counsel and advice about this season of your changes and the journey to seek reconciliation be aware of the fallen nature of all mankind. Not everyone who will offer advice and counsel in this situation will offer it without bias.

Their personal experiences with being offended or wounded by loved ones often have not been healed or their relationships have not been reconciled sufficiently to advise you correctly. With the understanding that those wounds and offenses can inform the advice given, ask God through the counsel of the Holy Spirit to enlighten those words of advice with His truth, mercy and love. Even with that caution, remember still that the other believers in your life have your best interest at heart and mean well. So do not totally discount what they have to say. Only the Holy Spirit of God can change any man's heart and heal the wounds of the past, so pray for all.

"And this I pray, that your love may abound still more and more in real knowledge and all discernment, [10]so that you may approve the things that are excellent, in order to be sincere and blameless until the day of Christ; [11]having been filled with the fruit of righteousness which comes through Jesus Christ, to the glory and praise of God." Philippians 1:9-11 (NASB)

Once you, your mentor and the Holy Spirit are in agreement about both the "who, what, how and when," then move ahead with seeking forgiveness and reconciliation with those agreed upon. The "who" is important, but what, how, and when are very important also.

As in a garden, the weeds must be pulled out or tilled under at the right time and in the right manner or the future fruit of the garden may be damaged or destroyed. One of the easiest methods of weeding a garden is simply to pull the weeds and unwanted growth out, roots and all, as soon as they appear. While that seems easiest and best for the entire growing season, it can be very destructive to the tender, young new growth in what the gardener wants to grow and produce fruit. That is also true in seeking reconciliation and forgiveness for the past sins and actions in your life.

Seek the guidance of the Holy Spirit and your mentor, and pray through each situation as well as discuss it with the heart of Jesus. A damaged relationship may, and often does, have many elements that have been damaged. The enemy of your soul and your life may have sown many lies into the past relationships. People interpret words, actions, and choices made through the "lens of their own brokenness'" and not simply the truth of what has transpired.

While your intent and desires are right before the Lord and others, the possibility exists for more damage to be done than good. Jesus' advice about "sowing" the word of God should be applied to this fragile, new growth and reconciliation from the past. Just because you are excited and filled with hope and expectations of good, does not mean everyone from your past is also. Be cautious and prayerful and seek counsel from the Holy Spirit and your mentors.

"The kingdom of heaven may be compared to a man who sowed good seed in his field. "But while his men were sleeping, his enemy came and sowed tares among the wheat, and went away. "But when the wheat sprouted and bore grain, then the tares became evident also.

"The slaves of the landowner came and said to him, 'Sir, did you not sow good seed in your field? How then does it have tares?' "And he said to them, 'An enemy has done this!' The slaves said to him, 'Do you want us, then, to go and gather them up?' "But he said*, 'No; for while you are gathering up the tares, you may uproot the wheat with them. 'Allow both to grow together until the harvest; and in the time of the harvest I will say to the reapers, "First gather up the tares and bind them in bundles to burn them up; but gather the wheat into my barn."'" Matthew 13:24 –30 (NASB)*

The advice of Jesus in this parable is sound advice for all of us in so many circumstances. If we think of ourselves as "slaves to Jesus" the Master and place ourselves in the current situation, trying to reconcile past damaged relationships, we can find our soundest counsel. Jesus has sown "good seed" into our lives through the desire of getting set free from the bondage we once were in. His word to us to seek forgiveness and reconcile our relationships is sound, but cautiously and carefully waiting until the right time and right way to harvest the fruit of His seeds.

What types of reactions can be expected when going to those on the list to seek forgiveness and reconcile? It is always wise to remember that this is a spiritual war and the unexpected should be expected at all times. Since the enemy seeks to "kill, steal and destroy" think about the various possible ways he could "kill, steal and destroy" the progress already made and the relationships that may already be damaged.

Praying and talking these possibilities through with the Holy Spirit, your pastor and your mentor should prepare your heart for the worst and the best. Whatever current level of freedom you enjoy, be prepared for the enemy to try his best to discourage you in these critical efforts. Remember the words of Jesus and live in the safety of the Body of Christ, as well as know God allows these trials to show us His power and to help us grow into the person He has planned for us to be.

"Therefore, having been justified by faith, we have peace with God through our Lord Jesus Christ, through whom also we have obtained our introduction by faith into this grace in which we stand; and we exult in hope of the glory of God. And not only this, but we also exult in our tribulations, knowing that tribulation brings about perseverance; and perseverance, proven character; and proven character, hope; and hope does not disappoint, because the love of God has been poured out within our hearts through the Holy Spirit who was given to us." Romans 5:1-5 (NASB)

The very best way to move forward in the things that may be painful and embarrassing is simply to trust in the Lord and not allow our own fears and imaginations to take control. Telling yourself it will be good for your mental, physical and spiritual well-being simply to move forward and leaning upon the Word of God is the only way.

"Trust in the LORD with all your heart and do not lean on your own understanding. In all your ways acknowledge Him, And He will make your paths straight. Do not be wise in your own eyes; Fear the LORD and turn away from evil. It will be healing to your body and refreshment to your bones." Proverbs 3:5-7 (NASB)

"Who is there to harm you if you prove zealous for what is good? but even if you should suffer for the sake of righteousness, you are blessed. AND DO NOT FEAR THEIR INTIMIDATION, AND DO NOT BE TROUBLED, but sanctify Christ as Lord in your hearts, always being ready to make a defense to everyone who asks you to give an account for the hope that is in you, yet with gentleness and reverence; and keep a good conscience so that in the thing in which you are slandered, those who revile your good behavior in Christ will be put to shame. For it is better, if God should will it so, that you suffer for doing what is right rather than for doing what is wrong." 1 Peter 3:13-17 (NASB)

Take some time now to pray, asking God what the very worst case scenario could be and then allow your mind to think about your worst case scenario and your greatest fear of what could happen and write it out.

_____

_____

_____

_____

_____

_____

_____

_____

As difficult as it may seem, the best way to move forward is simply to move forward!

As the time seeking reconciliation and forgiveness progresses, the very best defense possible and the most encouraging and perfect way to regain any lost peace is through prayer. The Holy Spirit will give strength as you spend time with Him and your mentor. Bear in mind that those who believe in Jesus Christ as Savior are no longer under the law of performance but now under grace. If times get too tough and your emotions get to raw, take some time away from this leg of your journey to total freedom and rest a while. Resting does not mean giving up, it only means you are following the Savior's example by stepping apart and seeking new strength and the voice of the Father.

"But Jesus Himself would often slip away to the wilderness and pray." Luke 5:16 (NASB)

Being like Him is our ultimate goal. Being prayerful and laying all your burdens at His feet can be one of the best actions to take. God wants to hear our hearts cry.

""Arise, cry aloud in the night at the beginning of the night watches; Pour out your heart like water before the presence of the Lord; lift up your hands to Him" Lamentations 2:19 (NASB)

One suggestion as you prepare for each of the times of seeking forgiveness and attempting to reconcile with those impacted by the past is to write out what needs to be said. Writing has been found to be very therapeutic and helpful in controlling anxiety and fears when facing stressful situations.

After writing out what needs to be addressed and going over it with your mentor, pray and continue to ask God what He wants you to address. Take some time now and write your list now and then pray, asking the Holy Spirit to guide your thinking and open His heart for you into your understanding of what to say and write.

_____

_____

_____

_____

_____

_____

_____

_____

_____

_____

Now spend some time in prayer with your mentor about what you have written. During this time of prayer, spend some significant time listening to that *"still small voice"* that God often uses in the life of a believer.

The battlefield of addictions to alcohol or drugs is often thought of as more damaging to the body and brain than behavioral aberrations because of the chemicals involved. As science continues to conduct research in this area, more is understood about brain chemistry and how the body repairs itself after damage or negative changes occur. The area most important for you to understand, now that you have looked at how nutrition and exercise, is something that can help overcome the damages done is the area of addictions to behaviors and how God has designed us to be renewed from the damages of those sins.

Finding freedom from behavioral prisons

Abundant Fruit that remains

"Now the whole earth used the same language and the same words. It came about as they journeyed east, that they found a plain in the land of Shinar and settled there. They said to one another, "Come, let us make bricks and burn them thoroughly." And they used brick for stone, and they used tar for mortar. They said, "Come, let us build for ourselves a city, and a tower whose top will reach into heaven, and let us make for ourselves a name, otherwise we will be scattered abroad over the face of the whole earth." The LORD came down to see the city and the tower which the sons of men had built. The LORD said, "Behold, they are one people, and they all have the same language. And this is what they began to do, and now nothing which they purpose to do will be impossible for them. "Come, let Us go down and there confuse their language, so that they will not understand one another's speech." So the LORD scattered them abroad from there over the face of the whole earth; and they stopped building the city. Therefore its name was called Babel, because there the LORD confused the language of the whole earth; and from there the LORD scattered them abroad over the face of the whole earth.
Genesis 11:1-9 (NASB)

From the beginning of time, mankind has made efforts to reach great heights with its own strength and through its own efforts. In this incident we see God's perspective on man's attempts to reach heaven on its own. We also see how God reacted to this desire of mankind to reach heaven and for individuals to be seen as extraordinary by others. His intervention may seem puzzling, knowing that He is loving and merciful.

Why would God confuse the universal language and spread mankind to the far reaches of the earth? It was so that mankind's continued conspiracy would be more difficult given they spoke different languages. Spreading mankind to the far reaches of the earth would require them to return to dependence upon Him and not strive for an extraordinary standing without Him. Those two very same issues are what lead to the prison of addictions, both chemical and behavioral.

No matter whether a person was once chemically imprisoned through drugs or alcohol and is now being set free or imprisoned by behavioral addictions without the chemical component, the obstacle that needs to be removed is the same. That obstacle is the thinking pattern that has been established that needs to be transformed, and God has the way.

"Therefore I urge you, brethren, by the mercies of God, to present your bodies a living and holy sacrifice, acceptable to God, which is your spiritual service of worship. And do not be conformed to this world, but be transformed by the renewing of your mind, so that you may prove what the will of God is, that which is good and acceptable and perfect."
Romans 12:1- 2(NASB)

Behavioral addictions, or what has previously been referred to in the first portion of this workbook as *"abhorrent behaviors"* are complex and difficult to overcome and difficult to be set free from. Using the term "complex and difficult" may be discouraging to many. It should not be discouraging because, like all changes that need to be made in lifestyles and behaviors, believers in Jesus have access to "divine power!" God created mankind and knew He would need to provide for the transformation He requires. We are created to have a way to overcome the sinful nature that has taken over us as His creation.

"In love He predestined us to adoption as sons through Jesus Christ to Himself, according to the kind intention of His will, to the praise of the glory of His grace, which He freely bestowed on us in the Beloved. In Him we have redemption through His blood, the forgiveness of our trespasses, according to the riches of His grace which He lavished on us. In all wisdom and **insight He made known to us the mystery of His will**, *according to His kind intention which He purposed in Him with a view to an administration suitable to the fullness of the times, that is, the summing up of all things in Christ," Ephesians 1:4b – 10a (NASB)*

God is willing and in some people has already unraveled the mystery (complexity) and provided the help needed to overcome the difficulties involved in addictive behaviors. This is true in of life's difficulties. That help is in the form of Jesus Christ and His provision *"In Him we have redemption through His blood, the forgiveness of our trespasses, according to the riches of His grace which He lavished on us."*

During the journey from freedom to addictions, both behavioral and chemical, the enemy of every soul, Satan, prevents mankind from seeing the truth about its journey. He will often throw a "spiritual veil" over our eyes to prevent us from seeing the reality of our choices. That veil can and will be lifted for those who choose to journey to the freedom once enjoyed. That lifting of the veil is because of the mercy of God who calls everyone to bring the things in the dark into the light.

"Therefore, since we have this ministry, as we received mercy, we do not lose heart, but we have renounced the things hidden because of shame, not walking in craftiness or adulterating the word of God, but by the manifestation of truth commending ourselves to every man's conscience in the sight of God. And even if our gospel is veiled, it is veiled to those who are perishing, in whose case the god of this world has blinded the minds of the unbelieving so that they might not see the light of the gospel of the glory of Christ, who is the image of God."
2 Corinthians 4:1- 4 (NASB)

The character of God is such that He uses the most gentle and merciful approach when we live outside His design. Like the people of old who tried to build a tower to reach heaven and make a name for themselves, God took the gentle approach by confusing their language and spreading them to the far reaches of the earth.

HE has already shown you His gentle approach by drawing you to Himself. Perhaps you are thinking that this journey wasn't as gentle and merciful as it could have been. Whereas we are free to make choices, even choosing outside of God's design for us, the consequences of our choices are often harsh and not gentle.

Never blame God for the harshness of our consequences and circumstances, when He was not consulted as to what the best choice was to make that lead to the situation.

Behavioral addictions are tied closely to chemical addictions in many ways. Seldom are individuals addicted to drugs or alcohol as a single form of addiction. Most are addicted to other drugs or alcohol, as well as behaviors that are outside of God's design for life. Pornography, sex outside of marriage, sexual self-gratification, homosexual liaisons if not pure homosexuality, gambling; the list is nearly inexhaustible. Once the freedom from chemical addictions is found and experienced through Jesus, the shame and guilt of the other types of sin become overwhelming and can cause serious problems in sustaining that freedom.

Now is the time to take an extensive look at what behaviors accompanied the imprisonment to chemical addictions. Set this workbook aside and make contact with your trusted mentor and friend who walked you through to this point in your journey. Ask for prayer either together or separately, seeking the Holy Spirit's revelation of what is not pleasing to God in your behaviors. Perhaps you already know. After praying and seeking the revelation needed to start the next leg of your journey to total freedom, spend some time listing those activities, behaviors and what became important to you dealing with stress and anxiety.

_____

_____

_____

_____

_____

_____

_____

_____

Again we find the definition of truth being an important aspect of freedom. One of the principle reasons mankind turns to abhorrent behaviors that displease God is an attempt to stop the pains of the past and present. The truth is these cycles cause more pain instead of stopping the existing pain. Many who find themselves in this destructive cycle come to the realization that the pain of continuing is greater than the pain of stopping.

That, like chemical addictions, must be the primary motivation. If you desire to stop these behaviors and break the cycle of guilt and shame, it must be because you, yourself, desire to break free from the prison. If you are seeking to stop because of someone else's urging or threats, while not all bad, it usually never lasts for long. In a commonly stated phrase – "You must be sick and tired of being sick and tired!"

While the behavioral addiction cycle typically cause painful consequences to many family, friends and other relationships, the internal pain and shame must be the primary reason to seek freedom.

*"Therefore I **urge** you, brethren, by the mercies of God, to **present your bodies a living and holy sacrifice**, acceptable to God, which is your spiritual service of worship."*
Romans 12:1(NASB) emphasis added

In today's world the world urge is often a word with gentle and oftentimes ambivalence attached to it. The word translated "urge" is actually a stronger instruction than many think, especially when it comes from God in His word. It is strong in the sense that it is more than just a firm and adamant suggested action. It is a firm and adamant suggestion and even more so **an on-going principle and practice** that is directly tied to what empowers us to be able, but also that is given from the Holy Spirit and expected to be followed in all things and throughout all our days on earth.

During the former life of being addicted to chemicals, if you were, the use of your body was simply a means to gain the so-called comfort and escape. If you had no addiction to ingested chemicals during the past, your "chemical or drug of choice" was internally manufactured. Escaping life's stresses and traumas through behavioral addiction is just as damaging to the body as ingesting chemicals, at times even worse; thus, the battle is just as difficult and just as possible, given the Creators design and power and His children's help.

How is that even possible, given the tough fight to overcome the use of drugs and alcohol? It is not possible in and of ourselves and our own strength, but not just possible with God's help, it is likely. Likely if we desire to complete the cycle of change and if we are willing to submit our wills and thinking continuously to the Holy Spirit.

What about the times when we don't seem to be able to hear from Him? Every follower of Jesus encounters those times and struggles with their thought lives. You are in the company of many who had the same struggle. The writer of the book of Hebrews was addressing this very issue to followers of Jesus who, in all likelihood, had either seen Jesus or knew some other who had firsthand experiences with Him.

"Therefore, since we have so great a cloud of witnesses surrounding us, let us also lay aside every encumbrance and the sin which so easily entangles us, and let us run with endurance the race that is set before us, fixing our eyes on Jesus, the author and perfecter of faith, who for the joy set before Him endured the cross, despising the shame, and has sat down at the right hand of the throne of God. For consider Him who has endured such hostility by sinners against Himself, so that you will not grow weary and lose heart." Hebrews 12:1-3 (NASB)

The question can never be, *"will God heal me?"* Rather it must be *"__will I choose to accept a sure and complete healing that Jesus promises, or will I reject it because of my doubts?__"*

"For sin shall not be your master because you are not under law but under grace." Romans 6:14 (NASB)

God created us so that the only thing that will truly satisfy us will be a deep intimate relationship with Him. When we search after love, acceptance and emotional nourishment in any other way or through any behavior the world offers, we distort the way that God intended us to live. Living in the fallen sick world, the only unfailing love comes from the only one capable of infinite love, Jesus.

". . what man desires is unfailing love". Proverbs 19:22 (NASB)

When anyone tries to quench their thirst through any form of abhorrent behavior or sustain their life through choices that are outside of God's plan, they are never truly satisfied. People spend money, time, and energy on what will not satisfy and will even cause more problems, when the solution is free. When anyone truly listens to God and His principles for life, He will commit to them for eternity.

"Ho! Everyone who thirsts, come to the waters; And you who have no money come, buy and eat. Come, buy wine and milk without money and without cost. Why do you spend money for what is not bread, and your wages for what does not satisfy? Listen carefully to Me, and eat what is good, and delight yourself in abundance. Incline your ear and come to Me. Listen, that you may live; and I will make an everlasting covenant with you, . . ." Isaiah 55:1 – 3(NASB)

Looking at the behavioral addictions that involve sex of any type that falls outside of God's design we find some of the "food" God spoke through Isaiah to warn us about.

Daniel L. Taylor

*Why do you **spend money for what is not bread, and your wages for what does not satisfy**? Listen carefully to Me, and **eat what is good, and delight yourself in abundance**. Incline your ear and come to Me. Listen, that you may live; Isaiah 55:2 – 3a (NASB) emphasis added*

Surrounded by media, filled with stress and coping with those stresses outside God's design causes most people to feel they are under attack, and they are. Given that "feeling" we need to remind ourselves that the enemy's goal is to – "Kill steal and destroy."

The power and pervasive nature of advertising with sexual overtones, movies with partial or complete nudity and the use of emotional language normally associated with intimate marital relationships is impacting society tremendously. Many of today's marketing experts use sex, instant gratification to life-long problems through chemicals, and the goal and desire for relaxation and pleasure accomplished through alcohol use and partying. With this constant barrage of instant fixes through chemistry and "no boundaries" sexuality in all areas of the media, young and old alike are acting out in sexually perverse fashion contrary to the design of God. Coupled with the proliferation of Internet pornography, government and business officials caught in sexual scandals, "the instant fix" mentality, a major pandemic of addictive behaviors is growing right before our eyes. Death and destruction inhabit a prominent place right in the midst of our society. Men and women alike in all segments of society, in all occupations and positions of authority, are finding themselves caught in the web of sin. All ignored or rationalized by a prolific trend of thought pattern and attitude which states – *"Character issues are less important than charisma and skills that produce gain"*. The guilt and shame that is hidden in their hearts behind apparent successful outcomes and charisma is often more solidly guarded and more deeply hidden behind the medicating effects of sex, drugs, or alcohol. Many men and women who are addicted to drugs and alcohol are also caught in the web of sexual sin. With all these named addictions and even more present in today's world, drug and alcohol addiction and sexual addiction are at the very core of the deterioration of our society.

The addictive cycle alone creates its cycle of pain, it continually hardens the heart and darkens the mind to such a great degree that if it is not interrupted, the end result is death, familial destruction or both. It only makes sense to first stop the cycle of "physical acting out" as an initial step in the journey to healing those in bondage. Sexual addiction, addiction to drugs and alcohol, and all other forms of addiction, once interrupted in the addict's physical lifestyle must begin by going through the period of detoxification. While the drug and alcohol addict encounters many unique physical manifestations in the detoxification process, every form of addiction detoxification follows the same or similar patterns and issues.

After the first few days of detoxification the process of discovering and understanding why they became addicted in the first place is an essential and vitally important early step in finding freedom. Once the repeated cycles of acting out are stopped and the physical and emotional detoxification is under way, and the core reason for the addiction can be discovered, it is then possible to go to the deeper issues of the heart and discover the keys to being free. "Being transformed by the renewing of the mind" (Roman's 12:2) is the one and only true way and paramount in understanding and living out how not to return to that destructive lifestyle. To begin with behavioral interventions only is fine, so long as the process moves rapidly toward a much deeper spiritual process that leads to true deepening of the relationship with Jesus Christ. Anything that falls short of that deeper spiritual journey will ultimately fail and will result in disillusionment and dissatisfaction with any future attempts at spiritual transformation. The ultimate goal of this study and the ultimate goal in every believer's life should be to find more and more freedom through Jesus Christ and to grow in all aspects of how God designed us to live.

This study is composed of countless experiences throughout the past 15 years, as well as reading everything written about addictions of all types. Those experiences along the road traveled on this journey of leading the ministry of the people of God have led to this destination, a home of eternal hope for all those addicted in any form.

While most of those cared for by the people of God are addicted to chemicals, or alcohol or multiple substances, nearly all have been found addicted to some sexually perverse behaviors or behavioral mindsets that displease God as well. The behaviors of those addicted to drugs or alcohol, as with those caught in web of sexual addiction, find common ground, much of which is can be best described as living from a distorted core of who they have become in contrast to the core of the way God made us to be. Coping with life's stresses through the use of substances, alcohol, or sexual sin boils down to one common element, not living according to God's design and from the true heart He gave us to live from.

The overriding goal of this study is to discover who God has made us to be, how and why we've distorted that through the addictive process that resulted from the use of drugs, sexual sin, alcohol and other coping mechanisms and returning to living from the heart He created within us according to the His original design. The end result is not simply to stop

Daniel L. Taylor

the acting out but also to discover how best to travel this life long journey of freedom and hope. Along that road we will, little by little, learn how God means our relationships to be lived out and how He would wish to restore us to the fullness of the relationship with Jesus as Lord and Savior.

Everyone living in any form of addicted lifestyle is doing so just to cover up their fear of truly being vulnerable and living in close, intimate spiritual and personal relationships with other people. Deep in the heart of most addicted people we find them truly fearful of that vulnerability and intimacy. Their mind's return to fearful patterns of thinking that if they allow closeness and intimacy according to the Father's design, someone may soon discover things about them that will be truly impossible to face. For many, choosing the path of addiction appeared to be the way to find safety and control when in reality there was a nearly total loss of safety and control. Everyone finding freedom from addictions must also find the ability to face all the possibilities and potential of connecting meaningfully to others. Ultimately, they must be willing to view themselves as worthy of love and acceptable before deep healing really begins.

If the addict is truly looking for complete healing above all else he must learn to receive love, become vulnerable and learn to embrace his own personal weaknesses and begin to dismantle the wall of false beliefs that he has hidden behind along the way. Learning to take risks as well as to trust, not just themselves but others and unlearning the self-defense behaviors is critical in finding freedom. Each person walking this journey must truly believe that God wants to heal him or her through the power of Jesus Christ, the healer of yesterday, today, and tomorrow. Standing transparently, bare of any self definition, completely willing to accept whatever happens through the sovereignty of God at the foot of the cross.

Head knowledge alone is insufficient to bring any lasting change in any person's life. Those who find themselves bound in the chains of addiction and who really want to change must be willing to press into a new life pattern no matter how much it hurts. That "pressing into" must begin with a transformed heart and a knowledge of who God made them to be. Once that "new hope" is found, even in part, the newly aligned heart directed lifestyle can be envisioned.

As the addicted person continues to spend their life and their resources satisfying their addiction, they begin to realize deep in the core of who they are, at the very center of who they've become; **nothing they have done or used truly satisfies**. That dissatisfaction coupled with living outside the design of Christ makes the motivated, sin sick addicted person a ready receptacle for the infilling of the Holy Spirit.

That infilling of the Holy Spirit comes when anyone is truly and totally surrendered to the Lordship of Jesus and truly and honestly seeks it from God the Father. The Holy Spirit will not completely purge the sins and enter into His fullness of filling anyone, unless it is what they desire most. Not the "gifts of the Spirit" but the true infilling of the Spirit without the expectations of His gifts. The gifts of the Spirit and the manifestations of God using the one who is filled are truly dramatic at times. Those who desire the gifts need to examine their heart closely and understand their true motivation to be filled with the Holy Spirit. Everyone must be constantly mindful of the fact that they are called "gifts" because they belong to God and not man. God will give those gifts according to His desires and plans, not man's desire and plans. Establishing the fact that God desires us first to be saved, then humble enough to know He is sovereign over all, then trusting that His plans are always best. The gifts will come, when He takes complete control and giving those gifts is completely according to His sovereign will and plan.

We know we cannot hide anything from the Lord nor can we hide anywhere from Him for any reason. Even when we try, He knows and He will often gently and quietly ask us a critical question. He did that with Elijah, His prophet, the man He had chosen to right the wrongs of the world his day and his own wrong responses to the situations he faced.

"*. . .The word of the LORD came to him, and He said to him, 'What are you doing here, Elijah?" He said, "I have been very zealous for the LORD, the God of hosts; for the sons of Israel have forsaken Your covenant, torn down Your altars and killed Your prophets with the sword. And I alone am left; and they seek my life, to take it away." So He said, "Go forth and stand on the mountain before the LORD." And behold, the LORD was passing by! And a great and strong wind was rending the mountains and breaking in pieces the rocks before the LORD; but the LORD was not in the wind. And after the wind an earthquake, but the LORD was not in the earthquake.*

"*After the earthquake a fire, but the LORD was not in the fire; and after the fire a sound of a gentle blowing. When Elijah heard it, he wrapped his face in his mantle and went out and stood in the entrance of the cave. And behold, a voice came to him and said, 'What are you doing here, Elijah?" 1 Kings 19:9-13 (NASB)*

Daniel L. Taylor

Stop and pray right now, asking God to reveal the truth about your desire for the infilling of the Holy Spirit. After praying sit quietly and listen to that *"gentle voice"* to show you what your heart truly desires – being filled with the Spirit or the gifts of the Spirit!

After spending some time in listening prayer, write out what you think you heard in your own words. Remember, there is no wrong response!

_____

_____

_____

_____

_____

Share what you heard and wrote out with your mentor and ask to pray together with you and ask the Lord the same as you did in private. The Lord loves it when two or more are gathered together in prayer, seeking His voice and His will.

Why now, after being set free from chemical addiction? Because of the enemy and his desires and what Jesus alerted us to!

"So Jesus said to them again, "Truly, truly, I say to you, I am the door of the sheep. "All who came before Me are thieves and robbers, but the sheep did not hear them. "I am the door; if anyone enters through Me, he will be saved, and will go in and out and find pasture. "The thief comes only to steal and kill and destroy; I came that they may have life, and have it abundantly."
John 10:7-10 (NASB)

Jesus greatest desires for all of us is: *"I came that they may have life, and have it abundantly.".* Abundant life is only found when freedom from chemical addiction and behavioral addiction is obtained through His mercy and grace, then being granted the gift of being filled with the Holy Spirit so those freedoms found in His abundant life can be shared with all we encounter.

The world is filled with men and women who have been set free from chemical addictions only to have limited freedom because of behavioral addictions and aberrant thinking. Those limitations can be lifted through purposeful choices, actions and healthy relationships with others who are God's people. The Church (not the building, the people) is the single most effective human instrument for healing, total freedom and for curing the social ills that are the result of the fall of mankind in the garden. That same *"army"* and its true soldiers who walk out their faith alongside those in bondage of any kind are used by God to defeat that enemy whose sole purpose is to kill steal and destroy life.

As you walk this journey out to total freedom and build relationships with pastors, mentors and the people of God, you will find it to be true. You will also find the battle against addictions of all kinds and the spiritual battle you encounter to, at times, get tougher. That is truth! !

The words of Jesus spoken to the woman caught in sin should be the words everyone who has been given freedom through Jesus' atoning sacrifice, constantly dwell on:

*"And Jesus said, "I do not condemn you, either. Go. **From now on sin no more**." John 8:11(NASB) (emphasis mine)*

Seasons of *Change*

Keeping this freedom for life

summary – conclusions - advice

By now you will notice a central theme to the principles in this workbook, Christ is all, your relationships with people of Christ is paramount to success and a continued look at the progress you have made thus far. Paul stated to those in Philippi who struggled.

"Finally, brethren, whatever is true, whatever is honorable, whatever is right, whatever is pure, whatever is lovely, whatever is of good repute, if there is any excellence and if anything worthy of praise, dwell on these things. ⁹The things you have learned and received and heard and seen in me, practice these things, and the God of peace will be with you." *Philippians 4:8-9 (NASB)*

This workbook should be used as a lifelong tool in the hands of the Holy Spirit. Staying faithful to being a part of an evangelical Church – having at least one other individual as a mentor and accountability partner – reading God's word every day – praying earnestly every day: allthese things are critically important to staying free.

Another very valuable practice and often the most encouraging thing anyone who has been set free from the prison of addictions is reviewing the answers you wrote in this workbook regularly, at least every year. That shows you in real terms the growth and maturity you are gaining - - or the lack of growth and maturity you have gained. The positive side of seeing real time how your beginning to go back to old thinking is that you have a choice, stop the backward slide, seek out your mentor and friends for help and submit yourself to the Holy Spirit through repentance.

The title of this workbook "***Seasons of Change***" and the analogy and comparison to planting and tending a garden are important. Each year a gardener applies the lessons he has learned from the various season of the year before. That way the gardener is learning from the past and improving the "fruit" that his energies produce and improving the nourishment from each seed that has been planted, tended and harvested.

As with the gardener, the "abundance" of that fruit will sustain their life, but also can be and should be given away to help nourish others. Now that you have this freedom, have learned from each season how best to keep improving the "fruit" of your efforts it is time to share that abundance.

Spend some time praying, talking with your mentor, your pastor, and the others in the Church you have faithfully attended during this journey and seek someone else who may need a mentor, friend and encourager. Bear in mind that being a humble, grateful and faithful servant of Jesus should always be foremost in our language and heart. While you are not an expert, you are now equipped to walk with another through their freedom journey. While you walk that journey out, the fruit of your "garden" can nourish them in many ways.

Spend the next few days in prayer and discussion with others, then write down the names of a few people who could possible use your knowledge, experience and encouragement. Bear in mind, the only safe relationship is a God honoring relationship, no matter the gender: it is strongly suggested that someone of the same gender is the only appropriate relationship on this journey.

_____

_____

_____

_____

_____

_____

_____

_____

_____

Pledge to remain free

I _____ before god almighty, my brothers and sisters in the lord, pledge to remain honest, transparent and faithfully committed to the freedom that god has provided.

My journey from this day forward will be one of honor, integrity and purity of heart, to the degree I am capable. When I know or even sense I am weakening and about to fall back into an old pattern of thinking or action, I will first cry out to god for help.

Should that not be the instrument used to bring me fully confident I can return away, I will cry out to my brothers and sisters in the lord who walked the journey of freedom with me.

No matter the cost to me, I will always remain in fellowship with a local church, the brothers and sisters in that local church and meet regularly in a mentoring relationship.

When the lord provides me with a sustained period of freedom and my local pastor believes I am ready to mentor another person into the freedom I have gained, I will boldly come alongside another brother or sister in need.

I have prayed and agreed with this pledge and all the elements contained within it, and willingly, freely and courageously place my signature as a covenant between myself, god and the brother or sister that has mentored me through this journey.

_____ date _____

Printed in the United States
By Bookmasters